all that

you can't

leave behind

A ROOKIE MISSIONARY'S LIFE IN AFRICA

by ryan j. murphy

FATHER'S PRESS

To contact Ryan Murphy:
email—rhmurphy@aimint.net
blog—http://strangersinkenya.blogspot.com/
web page—http://murphy.kijabe.org/

Cover photo and design: Mike Gaudaur

First printing, September 2007

Printed in the United States.

ISBN 978-0-9795394-1-1

Father's Press, LLC

Lee's Summit, MO
(816) 600-6288
www.fatherspress.com
E-Mail: fatherspress@yahoo.com

table of contents

ACKNOWLEDGEMENTS

Perhaps this book was born while I was sucking on a plastic straw in a San Diego McDonald's. As I sat there and told my missions pastor about the hundred and one dreams of a twenty-five year old newlywed, the burly blond in his late 40's listened intently with a smile on his face.

"I want to write," I said. Dream one hundred and two.

He paused for a second, searching for the most polite way to say, "What could *you* possibly write about?"

I didn't know. But as the conversation wore on, Brad Buser pushed me past dreaming about living to a place where my life would make a difference for the kingdom of God. Instead of merely being "interested" in missions, I decided then and there to give my life to God for full-time missions. And in doing so, I found something worth writing about. Thanks Brad and may you encourage many more to follow our Savior wherever He leads. And to all of the other pastors—Kenny, Eloy, Von, Rick, Ray, Jeff, Rick, Anne, Andy—thank you for helping us obey our calling.

I'd like to thank my wonderful wife Heather for being my partner in this life and my helper with this book. The seminal material of *All That You Can't Leave Behind* came from my blog *Strangers in Kenya*, which I began at the urging of Ian Fraser. Thanks Ian. I've had a slew of great editors along the way as well—my mom Cindy, my sister Emily, Kristy Faber, and Suzanne Geba. Mike Gaudaur did an awesome job with the cover photos and design. Thanks for sharing your expertise.

Thanks to Mike Smitley and Father's Press for caring more about the things of God than dollars and sales. I'll always be indebted to you for giving me a shot at sharing my story.

Of course, the biggest thanks of all go to my Lord and Savior. Thanks for redeeming this mess of a man and giving him more than he could have ever dreamed of.

Ryan J. Murphy

1

ONE
introduction

The world is not impressed when Christians get rich and say thanks to God. It is impressed when God is so satisfying that we give our riches away for Christ's sake and count it gain.
John Piper

I love reality television.

Before you hate me, hear me out.

I think reality TV shows are more than just a passing fad; I think they're here to stay. I think we're tired of trying to solve the same old murder mystery and sitting through a half hour of a laugh track-boosted sitcom. We want to engage, to be shocked, and to see something new; to experience life without scripts.

Shows like *Survivor* and *American Idol* feel kind-of real, and we like reality. Granted, "reality" has been heavily edited and condensed to fit into an hour time slot and most of the "real" people are three times more dysfunctional (or three times more beautiful) than anyone we know. But it still feels real, like there's no script.

Now, you may ask me how I know about reality TV. Aren't I a missionary in East Africa? I can't possibly have a TV over there, can I?

Well, I don't have network TV, cable, or a dish, but my friend Andy from Pennsylvania sends us recorded DVDs of our favorite shows, and we hook up our classroom LCD projector to watch them. While we might get our shows in the mail a few months after you've seen them, we still get them. I still get my occasional fix of reality TV even here in Africa.

Any other questions?

"Don't all missionaries live in grass huts, wear taped glasses, have 13 children, and stutter?"

My, my, my. I'm glad you picked up this book.

This book tells our story, the story of two American twenty-somethings who heard a whole lot of talk about reaching the lost and going to all nations, but didn't see a whole lot of it happening. Whenever there is a lot of talk about something, but little changes, it makes me ask two questions: *Are the talkers liars?* and *Why is nothing changing?*

We found that many folks were paying lip service to missions. I stood in churches where they would pray for the world to be reached every Sunday, but they would send none of their members and very little of their money.

This confused me. Were they praying for some pixie dust to fall from heaven and help these foreign people? Was there a real face to missions out there or was the American church mired in hypocrisy? In the end, I couldn't answer my first question.

The answer to my second question was two-fold.

One, real change *is* happening throughout the world, but where can the average Christian hear about such work? The non-partisan 6 o'clock news? Standing around the water cooler at work? Doubtful. The Gospel has been exploding throughout the world, mainly in places with very little money and thus very little international press to report it. But things *are* changing because of missions.

Two, the main vehicle that churches seem to use when it comes to "missions" are short-term mission trips with devout and passionate individuals who are often untrained cross-culturally. They are whole-heartedly committed to give a few weeks of their time to reaching the lost, and then they return to suburban living. If you study history, the real change, the powerful movements of God, began through long-term, career individuals who devoted not 20 days to a people group but 20 years; people who gave more than a few weeks of sweat; people who gave their entire lives.

My wife Heather and I felt this calling to career missions during college. It was one of the things that drew us together, and in our first 3 years of marriage everything we did was focused on this goal. Our budget, our teaching jobs, our church activities, our personal reading list—everything. We knew we wanted to teach the children of missionaries, but we had no idea where we were going. We hoped God would show us in time. But while we waited, we wanted to be ready. In the words of Uncle Rico from *Napoleon Dynamite*, we wanted to "do something while we were doing nothing."

So, we had it all mapped out. If we saved our money and disciplined ourselves, we thought we'd be free of our college debt in ten years (when we'd be in our mid 30's) and then we'd be free to go to the mission field. Paying off $50,000 in a decade sounded like an aggressive but doable plan.

God had a better plan. The housing market in San Diego went through a huge boom around the turn of the century, and if you've ever been there, you know why—beautiful beaches, plenty of cultural excitement, and 340 sunny days a year. Financial savvy is something I sorely lack, but lucky for me, I had friends. They guided me into the housing market long before it peaked, and in 2002 my wife and I were able to get a small house in a bad part of the city for a small, bad fortune ($260,000). We weren't exactly sure how the whole thing would play out, but we knew that while we worked toward our goal of going to the field, paying a mortgage made more sense than paying astronomical rent.

About a year later, lightning struck. A businessman from our church (upon hearing of our plan to become missionaries) said that he'd pay off $10,000 of our debt if we'd find a way to pay the rest. Neither of our parents could afford such an amount, but we knew of a way that we could.

Our house had appreciated nearly 20% that first year and was still climbing. If we sold our house, we'd be able to pay the other $40,000 of our debt and leave for the field. We took his offer and our ten year plan suddenly got pushed up six years by a financial miracle we didn't see coming.

The question of *How?* had been answered; next was the question of *Where?* We knew there were needs all over the world for teachers of missionary children. Wherever Americans are going, living and loving people for Jesus (and that's happening in most corners of the world these days), there is a need for someone to educate their children. We knew of two firsthand. Heather had been to Numonohi Academy in Papa New Guinea, and I had visited Faith Academy in Manila. Neither of us had ties to the third one under consideration, Rift Valley Academy (RVA) in Kenya, but we'd both felt drawn to it even before we knew each other.

We took our time and interviewed people from each school. We prayed about the vastly different ministries which our work would be supporting. After all, as teachers of missionaries' kids that's our real purpose—support. Help the missionaries do what they do by caring for and educating their kids. In the end, we felt like RVA was the best fit, and we were excited about devoting our futures to that school and those ministries.

Our parents and friends knew that we were headed in this direction for a long time (Heather's parents said they knew when she was still in junior high), so they blessed our decision, even though there was a new complication to factor in—our newborn son Micah. He was the first grandson on both sides of the family, and losing him was an extra sacrifice for all involved. All of our friends were in that baby-making stage of life, too, and there were no less than six other little boys within two years of Micah when we left. Theirs was a sacrifice as well.

Once we were officially accepted with Africa Inland Mission (the agency which operates RVA), we began raising support. You see, we may have been debt free once we sold our house, but most missionaries don't receive a salary. We are part of a "faith-based" organization which doesn't pay us a dime to travel or work; we rely solely on the Lord and His methods for providing for our physical needs. Churches, friends, family, strangers—He's brought all types into our support base.

It's funny how it took faith to step out on this ledge, but it was also faith that we found out there.

We worked all throughout this process. Heather taught history at a private Christian school in northern San Diego, and I taught English at a public high school in eastern San Diego. Our skills were honed in those first few years of teaching as we rubbed shoulders with amazing professionals and a diverse assortment of children.

Then, in our final few months in the States, we took some extra courses to prepare us directly for the field—the "Perspectives on World Missions" course put out by the U.S. Center for World Missions; a special education class and a technology course to keep our California teaching credentials up-to-date; and a language course at Mission Training International in Colorado.

The selling, buying, and packing stages were exhausting. We had not one but two yard sales (raking in over $2,000 for a disgusting amount of "stuff" we'd already accumulated in our short adult lives). Super donors helped us stock up on supplies which we then shipped in a container to Kenya, supplies which we were told would come in handy and would be hard to come by once there. We had to pack up and inventory our clothing and appliances and everything else which we felt we couldn't part with. That container then went by truck to New York, by boat to Mombasa, by train to Nairobi, and by truck to RVA.

It either came with us or was sold for seventy-five cents. Cars, furniture, TV, stereo…even our cat Moses—all found new homes when we left ours. We left nothing behind.

And that's about where this story begins, this story about all that you can't leave behind, about what you take with you no matter where you go.

But this story won't sound like anything you might expect. Missions work has changed so much in the past 100 years. My great-great uncle Dan was a missionary in Liberia in the early 1900's, and three years ago I got a hold of some of the letters he wrote to his brother. The letters had some element of conversation in them as they asked questions back and forth about each other's life, but the months which came between composition and reception of each letter made communication difficult. Months, though, have been replaced with minutes today, as the Internet and satellite phones have made the lives of missionaries much easier.

This is just one way that missions work has a new face. Travel is easier; airplanes and cars have replaced ocean liners and canoes. Anthropology has helped us respect and preserve cultures. Medicines help fight illnesses that killed missionaries previously. Past mistakes in planting new churches have improved current methodologies. Computers have assisted and sped up translation work.

The list goes on. My life in Africa is nothing like my great-great uncle Dan's. But many of the sacrifices are still the same. You can't step across cultural boundaries without going and moving and missing and giving and losing. You must sacrifice. There are no shortcuts to making lasting impacts on the lives of others.

If you're reading this book, chances are you want to make an impact. You want to engage, to do something new, and to shake up the world. To experience life without scripts.

I invite you to vicariously live through us in these pages. Enter our reality. Learn the lessons we learned. Cry our tears with us. Scream ridiculous shouts of joy. Feel the pulse of God's heart in Africa.

Then, put this book down and find your own reality. Your own part of the story God is telling throughout the world. Because, after all, it's His story and it's His reality that matters most.

And that's all that you can't leave behind.

TWO

the only way is the wrong way

I made my first book in 1st grade. I think it was about monster trucks. Although, now that I think of it, my first might have been about *The Dukes of Hazzard* TV show or WWF wrestlers—all subjects being equally book worthy. You name the subject, and I turned it into a book, even if the book's pages were only made out of Scotch tape and used-up elementary school workbooks.

Then in junior high I went sports crazy. I'd take old *Sports Illustrateds*, cut them up, and make my own magazines, featuring whichever sport was in season: basketball, football, baseball. I skipped the swimsuit issue, of course, because I was a serious journalist.

I started writing short stories and poetry in high school and found that compiling them into books for my friends was a cheap but unique Christmas present. People seemed to enjoy them, and I enjoyed not only sharing my ideas with others but also saving some moolah around the holidays. Cheap and unique—just my style.

Now, I'm a few years older, and the old desire is back. To write, to create, to make sense of all of the change that's happening in our little world. In less than one month it will be July 6th, and my wife, son, and I will leave for Kenya, embarking on a new career as missionaries who will teach other missionaries' kids.

But my purpose isn't singular. I'm not just chronicling my story for my sake. I hope to share these experiences and lessons with others, that others can see what mission work is like in the 21st century and join in the cause. So whatever this story ends up being, funny or heart-breaking, whiny or prophetic, sincere or cynical, I hope it teaches somebody something about the heart of God for the lost. That's my purpose for writing now.

And so another story begins…

*june 7—africa is the answer

As teachers of missionary kids, our missionary work looks a little bit different. We're not translating, teaching, healing, or working directly with the people we're living among; our mission is to help the kids of the people who are doing those things. One step removed.

So, our first big questions were A) where is the biggest need in the world and B) where are our hearts drawn to? Here's why Africa was the answer.

- There are 54 African countries and nearly 700 million people. 21.7% of the population has never heard about salvation through Jesus Christ.
- There are 771 people groups in Africa who have never heard of the Gospel and/or have no Christian church. (Note: the definition of "people group" is from the Greek word *ethne* and basically boils down to whom it is socially acceptable for you to marry.)
- Less than half of Africa's people have access to safe drinking water, leaving them exposed to water-borne diseases like cholera, typhoid and hepatitis.
- A third of the people in Africa are malnourished, and half live below the poverty line of less than $1 (U.S.) a day.
- Africa is the epicenter of the AIDS pandemic; more than 70% of people in the world with HIV or AIDS live in Africa.
- A quarter of all AIDS deaths in Africa are children.
- Without AIDS/HIV education, nothing will prevent it from spreading.

- Over half of Africa's population is under 15 years of age.
- The majority of these are orphaned due to the devastation of diseases such as AIDS which are rampant in Africa.

This is what breaks our hearts, what pushes us out of our safe zone, what can possibly bring us to move clear across the world. There are 771 people groups in Africa who have never heard the Gospel and/or have no Christian church. We want to be a part of bringing that number down. Millions suffer from disease and illness primarily because they're poor. We want to help them while they can't help themselves. Africa's children need food, medicine, shelter, education, and knowledge of God's love. We want to see their future be better than their present.

So we've volunteered, using the gifts and talents God's given us, to serve the missionaries who have the gifts and talents to help their futures, both here on earth and in eternity. That's how we fit into this puzzle, and that's why we're going to Africa.

*june 11—faith based

There are various ways missionaries are supported. Some folks are part of a denomination that provides a salary for the missionaries. I know of at least Southern Baptists and Lutherans operating like this. It's like a job. You apply for it, and if the denomination selects you, they pay you to do your work.

But a larger percentage of missionaries operate under a system called "faith based." This means that there is no steady income for them. Their support is provided by different individuals and churches. If God does not provide for them through the gifts of others, they might not be able to go and they might not be able to stay.

I kind of wish we'd be in the first group—salary provided and not a financial worry.

But we fall into the second category. We've been raising support since last September when we were officially appointed by Africa Inland Mission (AIM). Our support percentage climbed slowly all year until last week—the deadline. Time was up. If we didn't reach 100% by June 6 (a month before our scheduled departure for Kenya), AIM wouldn't let us go.

It was getting a bit scary. We were close. Very close. But we were still shy by about $300 per month. We didn't really have any leads on where the amount would come from. We had been speaking at various churches, but no one even hinted that they'd be supporting us.

Then we got this e-mail.

"Hi! We attend Hillside Community Church in Julian and have heard you share your ministry opportunities. Having had several nieces and nephews attend missionary schools outside the US we thank the Lord for your willingness to minister to both the missionary and their children. We would like to support your endeavor monthly. We will be able to give you $300.00 a month and will keep you in our prayers daily. The Lord bless you as you begin a new adventure.
Russ & Ida"

This was totally out of the blue. I don't remember talking to these people personally, and I had no idea who they were. But this was the final piece of our "faith based" support puzzle. Amazingly, it was for almost the exact amount we needed as well. One family took care of the remainder of our support need, all in one fell swoop.

Mission headquarters gave us a call shortly after this news and told us we were financially ready to go. The final hurdle was cleared. Now, all that is left is saying goodbyes.

*june 16—report card time

I quit my job two months ago. It wasn't the best thing for my students—losing their teacher and getting a new one midway through second semester—but I had to do it. We had so many speaking engagements and details to take care of that I wouldn't have been able to give them my best if I'd stayed.

If I were still teaching, I'd be working on report cards right now. So, rather than grade my students, I'm going to stop and grade myself. Take inventory of my thoughts and feelings these days.

Emotional report card for today: I'm awfully afraid. When I moved to San Diego at 18, no one was depending on me; sink or swim, I was basically the only one affected. Now, I've got a kid and a woman attached to me, and I'm responsible for them, and I'm going and schlepping them all over the globe. What am I doing? I can barely wash and bathe myself regularly, so becoming a cross-cultural missionary to Africa seems like a bit of a stretch. I'm fearful. As for Heather, she's never lived anywhere but SoCal, never been too far from Mom and Pops, and never gotten out of her little social circle. She has no idea what's coming, but she knows that it's coming.

Social report card: I'm starting to feel more and more like an alien here. People know we're about to go and so they don't know how to relate to us anymore. I can't imagine what it'll be like in four years (when we come home for our first home assignment). Not only will the city and churches change, but the people will change drastically, too. Four years ago, I had friends who were married but have since divorced, friends who didn't have any kids but now have two, friends who lived next door but now live states away, friends who were still in college, friends who weren't married yet, who attended different churches, who didn't attend church at all, and the list goes on.

A lot changes in four years. And in another four years, the tide will just keep on rolling.

*june 21—silent no more

I've been busy lately sharing with different groups— youth groups and small groups from churches all over the county. Speaking at the public high school where I used to teach topped them all, however. For so long I stood in the back of the Christian club meetings silently, the disinterested public employee who couldn't participate in "religious activities." Here was my chance. I got to share with the kids whom I care so much about.

My message is pretty much the same each time I speak. Obviously, I've got a bias for missions and the needs of the poor and hurting around the world, so it's a no-brainer that this will be part of my content. But my heart was further enlarged by a course that I took called "Perspectives on the World Christian Movement" put on by the U.S. Center for World Missions. These facts blew me away and certainly made my resolve that much stronger.

- Percentage of the world's population that calls themselves Christian
    - 0.1% in 100 AD
    - 1% in 1500 AD
    - 4% in 1900 AD
    - 9% in 1980 AD
    - 15% in 1992 AD
    - 33% in 2005 AD
- Number of languages into which the Bible had been translated
    - 1800 AD—67 languages
    - 2000 AD—over 2,800 languages
- Percentage of the world's population considered unreached
    - 1974—50%
    - 2005—33%
- In 100 AD, there was 1 church for every 12 unreached people groups. Today, there are over 650 churches for every 1 unreached people group.
- 95 cents of every United States church dollar stays in the US

- 75% of the missionaries in the world are working in countries that already are predominantly Christian; only 2% are working with the unreached.
- "Is it fair for anyone to hear the Gospel twice when some have never heard it?"—Oswald Smith
- "Suppose one of you has a hundred sheep and loses one of them. Doesn't he leave the 99 in the open country and go after the lost sheep until he finds it?"—Jesus

My message doesn't really have much to do with us, other than the fact that we're doing something to help. I know that the main reason people invited us to speak was because of this unusual and extraordinary thing we're doing, but it's not really about us. If it weren't for God and the needs of the lost, we wouldn't be going. It's far more necessary for people to know what's going on in the world and in missions than for people to know what's going on with us. We're not that cool.

*july 1—disappearing act

We had a few goodbye parties last week in San Diego. Everything was heightened by the finality of this visit. People see a little more clearly what their friends mean to them. Eye contact lingers a bit longer, words are said that are a little deeper, and no one really wants to be the one that walks away and finalizes the goodbye.

As our friends left though, it was eerie. Almost like that show (which I never watched but saw commercials for) *Without a Trace*. The person is there one second and then they disappear. One by one, they disappeared from our doorway…

In one sense, it was just another goodbye, like the kind you say every day. But, in reality, each goodbye was a kind of death. I don't want to over-dramatize anything, but the way I see it is that the person we said goodbye to last week will no longer exist. Pieces of them will look familiar in four years, and some of our souls have touched in ways that will last throughout eternity. But that person, in that place, in that relationship is—to put it bluntly—dead. What is born from now on is up to us. Whatever is born is our choosing. We stay as close as we want; we drift as far away as we want. But it's new from here on out. And so our friends and family walked out our front door, into the night. Gone, darkness, death.

New life is around the corner though. New relationships there in Kenya. New relationships made in new ways with old friends from the States. Next Wednesday the "new" officially begins.

* july 8—safely unaware

Our flight to Nairobi has basically gone off without a hitch. Grueling but smooth. First, we had a Wednesday night red-eye; then, a thirteen hour layover in London; and another night flight on Thursday. All things considered, it's gone smoothly.

But I'm forced to consider what could've happened, what could've gone wrong and changed our entire futures.

There might not have been rain in New Jersey, and we might have gotten into London an hour earlier. We might not have had to wait an extra 30 minutes for one family in our group to go through customs. We might have been better organized and ready to start touring as soon as we got to Heathrow. Any of these things could have drastically altered our futures. If just one of these things went differently, I might not even be typing now.

Shortly before 9 a.m. on Thursday there was a bomb on the Tube in London. A few minutes later various buses were also bombed. As I write, they've only confirmed 33 dead and 300+ injured. The totals will end up being much higher.

As I write, I'm in stellar health, listening to a John Reuben CD with my wife and one year old son sleeping soundly in their seats next to me in row 22. We're fine. Our family and friends have been contacted, and they know we're safe. Life is normal. Couldn't be better.

But, I ask again, what might have happened? What stopped us from being in harm's way? We were planning on being on the Tube and buses today at the exact time of a horrific and deadly act of terrorism. How is it that we're fine and millions of others are devastated by tragedy right now?

The Lord chose to protect us. He kept us out of harm's way, completely separate of our own wills and plans. There's nothing extra special about us that those victims didn't possess. It was just His choice. He has other plans for us. Perhaps tomorrow He'll bring us across another tragedy, a different emergence of evil in this dark world. Perhaps not. He'll be there when we need Him. Today though, I'm grateful that He chose to spare us at this time.

How often are we unaware of how fragile this eggshell life is that we live? And how unaware are we of the ways God's hand guides us in and out of daily minefields?

*july 10—the 7 hour church experience

Africa time. We'd heard about this concept at our orientation sessions; today we experienced it. *Eat rubber for breakfast every morning* was another maxim to help us adjust. In other words, be flexible.

Our seven hours at church today certainly stretched us. Unforgettable is a good word to describe our first Sunday in Africa with a sick 15 month old.

The bus here never breaks down, we've been told, but you can guess what happened at 8 a.m. Fifty missionaries and 20 Bible students stood around practicing their testimonies, songs, and their Swahili phrases while two vans (pickup trucks with benches in the back and a camper shell) shuttled us all over the region in place of the broken-down bus. At 9:30, our van departed to the church "in town." Forty-five minutes later we arrived at the church.

Needless to say, we were late. They waited for us somewhat (an extra hour of singing for both groups). The first group was a boys' boarding school adjacent to the church. We gave our testimonies in English to over 200 teenagers, and then the pastor preached. As we walked from the school to the local church, we were our own little white parade exiting through a friendly crowd of youth.

The church service was in Kikamba, and it was long—exaggerated even more so by a 50 minute offering to raise funds for a female Bible school student. We understood only the few things that were translated into English for us. Micah is sick with a fever and diarrhea. Heather and I were up last night from 1-5 a.m., still not adjusted to the time zone change. No breakfast. The benches were thin and wooden. The eleven o'clock hour passed, then the noon hour, then the one o'clock hour. Long.

The preacher gave a powerful message from Galatians 5:22 on patience. I think. It was a good word for us to be focusing on anyway. I got to give my testimony through a translator to the 150+ brothers and sisters there, which I pray the Lord blessed to my hearers. They then wanted to greet us with a lunch, and it was prepared by 2pm. We ate fast (which was a bit rude but was explained by our Kenyan host) since our truck had been waiting for 45 minutes to take us back.

We exchanged blessings with the elders, thanked them profusely for their warm welcome, and then piled back into the truck—Heather, the driver, and myself in a pickup cab with an exhausted and feverish sixteen month old across our laps. Forty-five minutes later we were back at the dorms.

The seven hour church experience. Africa time. Welcome to your new home.

*july 11—observations

Somebody told me to write down all of my first impressions of Kenya, that I'd soon become numb to them and wouldn't notice anymore. Here are a few.

- On the plane from London to Nairobi, whites were the minority and Americans were the super-minority.
- Two giraffe 500 yards from the airport exit. (What's the plural for giraffe?)
- They drive on the left side of the road usually, but more frequently they drive on the "good side" of the road. The good side probably wouldn't be called "good" in the U.S.; it'd probably get someone fired.
- When speaking at the Christian boys' school, the boys were quiet and respectful to me but talked while the ladies spoke.
- Car exhaust and open fires everywhere.
- Everyone stares. Few smile.
- Half completed concrete block buildings, filled with people inside.
- 22 people (including us) in a covered Toyota truck on our way to church.
- Duka is the word for a small store. Dukas don't have specific hours of business. People shop there whenever they are open.
- Days and nights are equal lengths close to the equator.
- Scratchy toilet paper.
- Prices are always negotiable. Sometimes they are higher if you are a rich mzungu (white).

*july 17—define "dirty" for me

I went to church in dirty pants today. I had gravy on my lower calf, splashes of chai on my front, smeared bananas on my thigh, and something sticky on my right shin. I preached a sermon in front of 100 high school girls dressed in filthy clothing. I wasn't dirty though, they tell me.

Having a 16 month old child always presents a challenge to personal cleanliness, but compound that with living in Kenya, and you're bordering on impossibility. There's dust and dirt everywhere you go, outside and inside. (In rainy seasons, that dust becomes a ruthless mud, I'm told.) But that's not the difficulty.

The problem actually lies in the garbage, or lack of it. Stick with me, here. There's no waste in Kenya. In the States, we have a well-established custom called "trash day." On trash day, people in trucks come by your street and throw in all of your trash, usually 2 or 3 bags per family. Then, they dump their trucks in an outlying region with millions of other people's trash. We have recycling too these days for our good garbage, and everybody feels so very eco-friendly about that.

Most Kenyans, though, burn their waste. They have a drum or just a small crater in the ground in which they burn everything that can't be used. Which isn't much. It's not real pleasant for your neighbors on burn day as your smoke fills their house, but they'll be getting their revenge when they burn.

So that's the macro explanation. The application: there are no paper towels, no napkins, and few trash cans. Sure, these disposable items exist here, but nobody uses them. They have hand mops for big messes, hand towels for medium messes, and the clothes they're wearing for the small ones.

Everybody is dirty here. I am dirty here. In the dorm where we're currently staying, there is an obvious lack of paper goods. Wash your hands in the sink and then you look. Spill a few drops in the kitchen and then you look. Your son slobbers on the floor and then you look. Have a runny nose? Nothing. There's not even a wastepaper basket in the bathrooms, if you even had a tissue.

I guess it's not a big deal, having dirty pants. But as a card-carrying Westerner, I feel I should confess. My name is Ryan, and I was dirty today, and that's…um…okay.

*july 20—the only way is the wrong way

(Disclaimer: The following may sound like the whining of a spoiled and privileged American male fighting to adjust to a third world country. And that they are. Given another few months, this will all seem so normal that it wouldn't be worth comment.)

Culture shock has been defined as trouble adjusting to customs which threaten your basic unconscious belief that you are right. Let me give you some raw glimpses of my first few days getting oriented in Africa, and I think you'll see just how "wrong" they are here.

Morning: The urinals look normal enough, but if you've got more serious business to attend to, they have holes in the floors. Brush your teeth in the sink, but bring your own water. (You did boil your water the night before, didn't you?) Otherwise, you'll be spending the rest of your day in the water closet. Don't plan on plugging in your razor unless you've got a 220 volt electrical adaptor.

Ladies must wear long skirts (at least to the shins), and men must wear pants. Rebel and your purity and dignity will be questioned. Breakfast is bread and jam. Every day. Don't get any jam on your hands though, because there are no napkins or paper towels here. Walking back from the cafeteria, make sure you walk on the left (not the right) side of the path. Yes, not only do they drive on the left side of the road, but they walk on that side too.

Afternoon: Walk 2 km. to the village as the crowded tuk-tuks (motorcycles with a bench on the back) swerve wildly and blow smog up your face. Exchange your currency at the local bank amidst a sea of beggars, cripples, and drunks. Then, take your shillings to the market under the watchful eyes of hundreds of natives. Convert the cost of everything into dollars for yourself before you buy. Watch out for the metric system. Buy your gas in liters, your potatoes in kilograms. Wash your fruits and vegetables in bleach (and even then it's risky).

Since there are no phones, you try to communicate with your family via computer, but the Internet cafe attendant has decided to take a break. You try back an hour later, but now you've forgotten to charge your laptop. You don't have the 220 adaptor still, so you'll need to return to the dorm (stay on the left side of the path) to find an unused one to borrow. Three hours later and on your third trip to the cafe, the Internet (which is already deathly slow) has crashed. Come back tomorrow to see if it's up and running.

At twilight, all of the Africans are outside visiting each other, staring at you. You smile back at the men and say "hi." They just stare. You kindly wave to a woman, and she ignores you. You find out later that in their culture you were flirting aggressively with her. Be careful. (Why don't the mosquitoes bite them like they're tearing into you?) The weather has cooled off to 24*C, whatever that means.

Evening: You arrive five minutes late for dinner and two of the three main dishes are gone. Leftovers are not a tradition here, not even in cafeterias. They've estimated a bit short, and so your stomach will have to thrive on mashed beans and water. There is a snack bar, but no hours are posted on the window. Unfortunately, it's now closed. As you walk back to the dorm (on the left side remember), you look to the skies. Even the stars are not familiar—you are in the Southern Hemisphere.

Your entire family sleeps in one room. The beds here are built to last, not to comfort. They're foam, but not like foam cushion. More like Styrofoam. (I'm serious.) The pillows are foam too.

We'll see you at the first crow of some overachieving rooster (probably 5am). Have a good night.

Sleep.

*july 21—aids

Perhaps one of orientation session I was looking forward to the most was today's on HIV/AIDS. I wanted the ground floor perspective. What was even better was that I got a Kenyan AIDS worker's perspective. Here's what he shared.

- It's tough to get accurate statistics on AIDS. The only cases which can be determined are the people who are tested—usually only pregnant women.

- In the U.S., women make up only 25% of the AIDS cases. In Africa, it's almost 60%.
- Main causes of the spread
  - Wife sharing—the belief is that it's better to have babies by different men to avoid a curse
  - Wife inheritance—widows are taken in by wealthy older men
  - Circumcision—rite of passage for new teenagers. Same blade used for many during the ceremony. Female mutilation is still practiced also.
  - Early marriages—young girls with older men.
- Basic treatment for HIV/AIDS is $40 per month. Advanced treatment is $90. (The average Kenyan makes $30 per month.)
- Faith healers tell AIDS patients they are healed. For the healing to work, the person must have faith. In faith, they go off medicines and go on with life as if they were healed.
- Superstition that if you have sex with a virgin (even a toddler) you will be cured of AIDS.
- Heavy stigma and secrecy associated with the disease. It's a relief if someone is actually dying of cancer instead. Sometimes that lie is told to hide the shame of AIDS.
- Women will be kicked out of home if they are diagnosed and shunned by their community, even though it may have been the undiagnosed husband who gave HIV to her.
- Orphan girls will sell sex for 20 shillings (a quarter U.S.) and then contract HIV and die. Poverty drives HIV.

I wonder how long it will be until I see, feel, experience the AIDS suffering here. I know my primary ministry will be to missionary kids, but I'm living in a country now where 1 in 5 adults has it. Probably a better question than "How long until?" is "Whom will I love with AIDS?"

* july 23—God is still speaking

I skimmed through a book the other day. It was a couple hundred pages long, and the introduction boldly announced that God began talking with the author one day. All the author had to do was write down what he was told, and *viola*, this book was the result. It was a *New York Times* bestseller, spawned sequels, and made him a boatload of money. I forget his name, but the book was called *Conversations with God*.

It's a fascinating topic though, really. Does God still speak to people? If so, how much, to whom, how frequently… the questions go on. I'm not sure how many people in the States even believe he does. Some.

Many ancient peoples have claimed to commune with God. From Middle Eastern cultures to the Americas to the Far East, our ancestors have learned much from the spirit world, for sure, but few have claimed to commune with the one, all-powerful, all-knowing, creator God. This, according to any continuous historical record we have from an ancient culture, began with the Hebrews.

God spoke a lot at the beginning to these people and for good reason. There are millions of gods out there, and He needed to introduce himself. He didn't have a resume or a website, so He told them who He was, often at lengths. They carefully recorded these words, memorized them, and passed them down.

But, as time went on and God's fame and reputation spread, He didn't need to speak as much. Usually He just picked out one or two people to speak with at any given time. There was even a time when He stopped speaking all together, according to Jewish and Christian historians: the 400 years right before Jesus arrived.

What is so amazing to me is the consistency of God's message through Abraham and Moses and Isaiah and Jesus and

Paul. There are mysteries along the way and confusion, granted, but the overall message is consistent. Worship God. Faith alone will save you. Love your neighbor. Obey God, and you'll be blessed. Something like that.

As I try to discern among all the other people out there who have "spoken with God" or "heard God's voice," I try to keep this consistency in mind. Does it sound like the one God who revealed himself steadily for thousands of years in the cradle of civilization and appeared as Jesus? Or is it a bit fishy? Does it contradict prior "words" from God? If "the voice of God" openly attacks a specific faith, like Judaism or Christianity, I'm immediately certain that it's not the voice of God.

Muhammad heard a voice. It said that our rituals could save us, Jews and Christians were damned, and all kinds of other things. Muhammad wasn't sure if it was God or a demon though, and he admitted this. Ask any Muslim scholar. Nevertheless, millions and millions follow this one man's testimony of the voice.

Joseph Smith heard one too. His said that the church had gone astray, Jesus wasn't God, and it's all right to marry many wives (although his church has since changed this particular "word from God"). His voice told him about a lost tribe of Hebrews who landed in America and hung out with a spirit Jesus (even though millions of dollars spent by the LDS church has still yet to produce one artifact or relic from this "historical" people group). Again, millions follow the one man's testimony to the voice.

Conversations with God is nothing new. I'm not disputing that this guy heard a voice, but I know, because of that voice's inconsistency with the voice of God in the past, that this wasn't the real God speaking.

Let me tell you how God spoke to me...

*july 24—more than useless

They told us that our son Micah would be the first missionary when we got to Africa, and they were right. If his wispy blond hair, chubby belly, and cherubic cheeks are magnetic for Westerners, they are virtually irresistible to the Africans we've met. Thirty teenage girls on a school field trip mobbed him outside of Nairobi while we were waiting to get on a bus—pointing, giggling, poking. Luckily Heather held on to him tightly.

It's no different here among the missionaries and their children. We can't walk to the dining hall without a dozen people or more saying hello to Micah or asking him what sound a cow makes or trying to tickle him. People love babies just because. They don't really do anything. You could even call them useless or helpless if you wanted to.

In my eyes though, Micah is a prince. I absolutely love holding him in my arms while people dote on him and enjoy him. I'm so proud of him, for the ways he's already grown, for his personality, and for who he'll become. But basically, I'm just plain proud.

Why do I go on with these universal thoughts and feelings of parents everywhere? Well, a few nights ago God used these very emotions to speak to me.

Already feeling jet lagged and afraid of my new home, I woke up one night at 1 a.m., not to go back to sleep. I went to an empty room and read a book for a while. Then, I paced the room and prayed for while. 4 a.m. No rest, still troubled.

And that's when God spoke. It wasn't an audible voice, although He occasionally speaks to other people like this. It was in a way that He's spoken to me a few times in the past. The best way I can explain it is as a thought in my head that is in a different voice than my thoughts normally take. It came at a time when I was asking God a question. Its timing was off; its clarity rang out. When it came, I knew whose it was.

The question I asked was: How do You see me? I was feeling empty, useless and lost, and proportionately, did not have a very accurate perception of myself. He didn't answer immediately or maybe I just didn't hear right away. But this is what I heard.

I feel about you the way you feel about Micah, and the precise picture of me holding my son and all of the emotions I feel at that moment hit my heart at once.

Here I am, a baby to the new culture I'm learning, lacking identity, lacking the ability to live on my own here. Too tired to walk, too weak to make it. God is carrying me through, and my strength is gone. I'm useless.

But then He tells me, "I feel about you the way you feel about Micah," and I'm more than useless. I'm loved. I'll be able to go a long time on those words.

*july 26—i like to move it, move it

Africa Based Orientation (ABO) wraps up today. Tomorrow we take a bus west to Nairobi, eat lunch, and then head farther west to RVA to set up our apartment and begin our orientation there.

ABO was good because of....

- The classes (wide variety of topics—AIDS, African culture, the African church, dealing with corrupt governments, interpersonal relationships, grieving, personal health issues, etc. Tons of information in 18 days).
- The cultural exposure (we got to ease into currency, travel, food, churches, communications, climate, etc. We feel much more ready to head into Kijabe and learn about that culture and people).
- The people (we met other missionaries from all over the globe who will be traveling to six different countries doing many different ministries. This time really helped form a "team" with others in our diverse organization).

ABO was tough because...
- The pace (jam-packed with classes. Not enough time to process and to be with our family).
- Our health (Micah had a cold, was teething, had some stomach issues, and didn't sleep well. Thus, we didn't sleep well and got sick).

Overall, we're pretty wiped out, and we want to head into our new hometown with energy and excitement for settling in and learning everything we can. Our life is so up in the air right now and on top of that, we find ourselves missing many different things and people. But we're glad ABO is over, we're glad these hard months of transition are over, and we can't wait to start doing what we came here to do.

THREE

eating an elephant

AUGUST-OCTOBER 2005

As I said in the first chapter, our story really isn't that unique. We're just straggling behind the thousands of others who have been strangers here. The really unique story happened in 1895, when a handful of missionaries packed up a few possessions in a wooden box (purposefully and ominously large enough to be a coffin one day) and followed a life calling to bring the good news about Jesus to the heart of Africa. The coastal regions of the world knew about Christianity already (through European traders mostly), but the interior regions of Africa, China, India, etc. were unreached. Most of these early missionaries to Africa returned to America or the UK shortly after in their boxes, but their deaths didn't stop the vision. More went in their place, and Africa Inland Mission was on its way.

Thanks to the railway from the East Coast of Africa on the Indian Ocean, which was built a few years earlier, the mission was able to get a head start on its inward march. Trailblazer Charles Hurlburt knew that it needed a base to start operations, and he found some land to buy from the British in Kijabe. I'll tell more of the peculiar details of God's providence in this purchase later.

As more missionaries started coming to Kijabe and farther west, there began to be quite a population of little white people. Children. What was to become of them here? Was their education to be neglected? Were parents supposed to forget about their work with the natives and educate their own children instead? Were the parents qualified enough to do that even if they wanted to? It was a predicament. Parents feel called to reach the lost. Parents have kids who need education. Nobody had looked quite that far into the future. And if they had, then the decision was to literally sacrifice their children's futures for the sake of the lost.

But Hurlburt knew of a lady in the US who was gifted with children and also was interested in being a cross-cultural missionary—Miss Josephine Hope. In 1906, she came to Kijabe and began teaching a handful of children their primary lessons. That was the start of what is now known as Rift Valley Academy, and it's been going strong (more or less) for the past 100 years.

AIM, the agency that we are working under, has over 850 missionaries in 15 African countries and in some islands in the Indian Ocean. The ministries are vast, from doctors to church planters to pastoral preparation for Africans to community development, and they continue to spread to wherever people are unreached. The original goal of evangelizing all the way inland to Lake Chad was reached, but there are still many areas that remain unreached, especially the Muslim regions of Northern Africa.

RVA operates under the umbrella of AIM but serves over 70 other mission agencies that work in Africa. All told, students at RVA come from 21 different countries, but it hails as an American school, accredited under Middle States Association. There are about 500 students here in grades 1-12 although most of the students are in high school, thanks to the recent trend of home schooling little children as long as possible. The missionary staff is completely voluntary. Not one of us gets a dime from the school or tuition or anything. We're all financially supported by faith to be here, and it's operated like this for over 100 years.

That's what we're doing here at Rift Valley Academy. That's how we got here. An incredible story that we're simply adding a few short sentences to.

*august 2—e.t., i'm feeling you

We're settling into our apartment this week. Our container won't arrive for another month or so, so we're living with what we packed in our suitcases and with rental furniture and appliances from the school. It's nice to have our own bit of space and let our guard down finally, knowing that we'll be here, within these four walls, for a while. But there's one thing that beats everything else at this point in our adjustment: the ability to communicate with loved ones.

I don't know if this means I'm homesick (maybe a bit) or if I'm avoiding diving into our new relationships and culture (I don't think I am), but it's just such an encouragement to be thought of, remembered, reached out to from across many, many miles. I feel like that awkward, raspy alien, gurgling the only thing that was on his mind, *E.T. phone home.*

I'm loving life here, the challenges and adjustments of a slower pace, learning the history of British colonialism and Western missions work and how that affects current relationships and ministry. It's not all bad. Similarly, E.T. liked Reese's Pieces, living in the closet, Eliot, and Eliot's foxy sister, but it still wasn't home. He had to get in touch with his loved ones.

We've gotten a few calls on our new Kenyan cell phone of dubious quality. (Our old American cell doesn't work here. The rest of Europe is just fine using theirs anywhere in the world, but not us. Go figure.) Our conversations have been cut short a few times and are very staticy, but that's not the point. The point is that I've heard voices of friends and parents and siblings who mean the world to me.

We don't check email every day, but almost every time we've checked it, there's been a little note from someone who misses us or is praying for us. That's just great. Just yesterday we got our very first postal mail from the States, and it only took 16 days to get here. Sweet. It's nice to know that we haven't been forgotten, and that the team that sent us here to do this work is functioning at full tilt. Not every missionary gets this kind of encouragement today, and historically, monthly contact was sometimes a rare phenomenon.

Although I can't frequently call the States from here (it's about a buck forty per minute) and I shouldn't take the time away from my training and work to write lengthy letters and emails, I'm so grateful for every contact that people have made with us. While I'm working in Africa, I am striving to find the balance between staying "in touch" and staying (emotionally, relationally, mentally) "in America." But it would really help if someone sent me some Reese's Pieces while I'm looking for it.

*august 6—the american within

I mentioned that some thoughts and observations were coming about money in Africa. I'm not ready to write those yet; there's still too much percolating within. I'll give you a preface, though, with this song by rapper John Reuben. It's very satirical (the chorus is "Puff the Magic Jesus") and very hard-hitting at the same time ("ignore the crying outside your door"). Money. How do we deal with it?

Puff the Magic Jesus floats around the universe
The United States is his favorite place on the whole entire earth
So sing your songs and wave your flag
And thank the Lord for all you have
But what about them? Did you forget about them?

We came, we conquered, never speak of this again
Life must go on, let's not think of them
Things are comfortable now, the pioneers have settled in
Perfect blend of progress and pale skin
What a prosperous, wondrous place
Remember to say grace before we scrape our plates
And ignore the crying outside our door
Sure, you'll pray for their burdens but you don't want to make them yours

The more you have, the less you care
The less you care, the more you become unaware
God bless us as we sweep this mess under the rug
Don't want to walk barefoot off the tile and step in the mud

Out of sight, out of mind, pushed to the side
Left for someone else to rationalize and justify

*august 9—things that go bump

I haven't been sleeping well in our new home. I'm not normally scared very easily. Back in the States I'd be the one who'd be awakened out of a deep sleep to go check on something my wife heard in another part of the house. I did it to calm her worries, not because I really feared anything was wrong. That has changed in Africa.

Security and safety have a slightly different feel here. You have to take extra precautions to get to that place where you've done all you can and you can rest. Our windows have bars on them, our two inner doors have regular locks, and our two outer doors are metal gates with padlocks. You want your curtains drawn at night and all your valuables out of sight.

I should probably go back a step further. Since we live on a boarding school campus, there are ten foot barbed wire fences around the perimeter of campus (about a mile's worth) and three gates with multiple guards and dogs at each. The reason for all this is that during school there is a slew of kids on campus, and if parents are going to leave them here while they're hundreds of miles away (or more), they want them safe.

So is it really that dangerous here? In a sense it is. There's really no random violence here; it's mostly motivated by money. The poorest Westerner is a king in the African context. Within this missionary community at RVA, the average person in Kijabe sees a goldmine. The school's chaplain forgot to lock his outer gate one Sunday morning, and while he was predictably at church, a burglar took an axe to his inner door and made off with a loot of electronics. Yes, this was inside the fences.

Even the kids who live here are rich, so they also are targets for theft. A female soccer player was running just outside the gate and was accosted. She didn't give the man her CD player, so he hit her and took it. She was separated from the group, weaker than her assailant, and possessing something that was worth two months wages for an employed Kenyan. Easy target.

Okay, let's get back to me being afraid of the dark. Your big sissy narrator. We live below a 7th grade girls dorm with no carpet and cement all around; hence, serious echoes. We live on the side of a mountain; hence, serious wind. We live at the very bottom of campus, right next to the lower fence, and we can hear the sounds of the town just below. It's pitch black outside. Our pipes creak. Until school starts, the dorm is completely empty, so the nearest person is five minutes away.

And, wouldn't you know it, every night as I'm drifting off to dreams of cheeseburgers and freeways and my idyllic home country…boom.

My old house in the ghettos of San Diego had nightly helicopter searches, high speed police chases, and drive-by shootings, all within two blocks of my house, but afterwards, Heather and I'd always fall back asleep pretty quickly. For the time being though, the things that go bump in the night keep me up for hours. *What was that sound? Was it inside the house? Did it come from Micah's room? Is the tennis racket in my closet really my only means of defense? I hope Heather still remembers Tae Bo.*

I trust God to protect us. I really do. We need to be smart, be diligent, and be aware of anything suspicious, but beyond that, our safety is in His hands. Many people are never mugged here, and most people never have their houses broken into. Those who are or do count it as part of the cost of loving people for Christ, sharing in His sufferings in some small way. And all the rest of us pay a little bit of this price with a constant,

low-grade sense of danger and the occasional sleepless night.
I'm just paying my dues.

*august 10—settling in

We've been in Kijabe two weeks now and are very glad
to have a two bedroom apartment to call home. We're enjoying
a few more weeks of quiet before the 13-year-old-female-army-
of-energy arrives to the dorm above us.

We found out our probable teaching assignments. I'll be
teaching English to the 8th and 10th graders. Each class will be
around 25 kids, so I'll have two periods of 8th and three periods
of 10th. Heather will either be teaching 9th/10th World History
or junior/senior Modern European History. You can probably
guess which one she's praying for considering her teaching
experience is with younger kids, but she'll gladly help out
wherever needed.

We began our language sessions this week and are
trying to get as many in as possible before the school year
begins. All the Kenyans laugh when we say we want to learn
Kikuyu. Very, very few wazungu (whites) have become fluent
in Kikuyu through the years. They even joke that wazungu
can't learn it. It's more challenging than Swahili but not nearly
as tough as English.

Our container with all our belongings has an ETA of
August 23, but that is an "estimated" time. It could take weeks
longer. We're renting most of our furniture and appliances for
the time being from the school, which is a nice temporary
solution. Salim, a local craftsman, is making a few pieces for us
out of mahogany (one of the three available woods in Kenya),
and the rest we'll be purchasing or ordering over the next few
months. We're grateful for the outgoing funds that were given
to us by supporters in the States, as now we're finding good use
for them settling in here at RVA.

I've been getting to know some of the students and staff
through tennis and basketball, but I hurt my ankle very badly on
Sunday night (probably sprained, hopefully not broken). This

means double work for Heather around the house and with Micah, as I'm immobile right now. I'm going to get it checked out before the weekend at the local hospital.

*august 12—smoking machines

As you may or may not know, most of the non-American world uses 220 voltage, not 110. Well, we were told we could simply plug our computer into the power here on campus because computers can handle different levels of voltage.

Bad information.

A loud, firecracker-like sound and billows of smoke resulted. The tech guy Jeff said the power supply got fried and that when it gets replaced, the rest of the computer should be okay. ("Should" really isn't good enough when you're talking about all of your documents and emails and files and music, but it's all he could give us.) He then tried to find one in Nairobi but came up empty. 400W is the largest output he could find and we need 550W.

Our computer isn't as essential as oxygen or food, but with school coming up, it'd be nice to get it up and running ASAP. We sent an email out to a few dozen people asking for help. I asked them to package it well and put it in a plain brown box. At the post office, they simply need to write "power supply" on the customs slip and the garage sale value of the item, not the actual. That way it won't attract any potential thieves. The shipping cost will probably be around 30 bucks, and it will take about a month to get here.

Getting things done here is a little different than going to your local computer store after work, installing it before dinner, and surfing the net again by evening, isn't it?

*august 18—eating an elephant

Although we live at 8,000 feet altitude, there have actually been elephants wandering around these forests. Sometimes the Kenyans have to kill them because they'll trample crops and become dangerous to the town folk. It's hard for me to imagine; they seem like such a majestic species and all, but if they threaten your livelihood or your well-being, I guess it's a must. The other night they tell me I had my first taste of elephant.

Well, not real elephant. Metaphorical elephant.

Have you ever heard the adage, "How do you eat an elephant? One bite at a time"? That's the analogy we've been taught when it comes to learning a language. From first glance, it looks much too big and overwhelming to be done. But if you take it little by little, bite by bite, you'll get there.

Priscilla Muhota is our first language helper. She's a student on break from Nairobi University, speaks English beautifully, and is a native Kikuyu speaker. After an hour with her, it felt like we were idiots and had accomplished virtually nothing, but it was a start. Our first taste of elephant. Here are a few things we've learned about language learning so far.

1. **It takes a million mistakes to learn a language**. This takes a lot of humility, to become like a baby again, and it's hard for educated individuals to accept being totally and utterly ignorant. Our friend Andrea has this kind of humility. She started to learn Kamba (the language of a tribe in Eastern Kenya) and greeted a group of boys outside of a church with *wachaa*. Unfortunately, there is another word, *wacha*, which is a command meaning "leave." We then understood why the boys became sad at her supposed greeting. Mistake #1 of a million—she's on her way.

2. **You have to murder the language before you master it**. As an English teacher, I help murderous children become less brutal and more masterful with their use of the English language; now though, I'm on the murdering end. There's a story about a man who was learning Mandarin. He was riding a bus home one night with his family, exhausted from a night of visiting friends. As his stop approached, he quickly grew afraid that the driver might go past and they'd have to walk many blocks to their home. He quickly yelled,

"Cha ji." The passengers looked at him quizzically and then began to laugh. He should have said, "Shia chi," which means "stop the bus." Instead, he told the bus driver to kill a chicken.

3. **Learning language is great way to build relationships.** Whenever we tell native Kikuyu speakers that we intend to learn their language they laugh joyfully at the thought. They feel honored that we care enough about their tribe to undertake such a momentous project. Thus far, I haven't come across anyone who won't teach me a word or phrase willingly when I ask. One more story. A woman was having car problems in a Latin American country. When she pulled into the garage, she got out and exclaimed assertively, "My car won't start. Please change the points." Or so she thought. What she actually said was "My car won't give birth. Please change the bananas." The mechanic had a good laugh at her expense, but he became a lifelong friend because of this memorable encounter she had with him.

They've also told us that learning a second language is like gaining a second soul. Outgoing people become more reserved in a foreign country, and the shy become bold. Something changes inside of you; you become a child again in many ways and you grow up into an adult again.

Heather and I are growing up Kikuyu now, and the only way to grow up big and strong is to eat your elephant, one bite at a time.

*august 20—fast responses

When God comes through for you, it's impossible not to praise him. It's effortless. First of all, many responded to the computer power supply need, which gave us a few options. The best one is a new missionary who is coming next month. He's going to pick one up and bring it by hand, saving us $30 postage. Sweet!

Secondly, our shipment arrived from New York already! Five weeks is a record from the States to Nairobi. We weren't expecting it until September at the earliest. But, like the Grateful Dead say, "Every silver lining's got a touch of gray." The shipment may have gotten here a little too fast. We need our e-permits (kind of like a green card in the States) to be cleared by the Kenyan government so that we can receive our shipment through customs. We applied for them seven months ago, which you'd think would be enough time. Sometimes they clear quickly; often, they do not. There's no rhyme nor reason; it's just how it is in Africa. No e-permit, no receipt of shipment. If you can't receive it, it sits in storage at the cost of $100 per day. Ouch.

*august 22—take up your crutches and...

Giddy. There's no other way to describe it. Walking home from the training room without pain, carrying my crutches, the sun on my face, the flowers beaming their bright colors. No, I haven't been eating any hallucinogenic African herbs. I was healed.

I'm ahead of myself though. Let me start at the very beginning (a very good place to start). I had been laid out all week by this sprained ankle. About the time when I should've been able to start putting weight on it again, I started to feel a piercing, pins-and-needles pain in my foot. Uh oh. Broken bone. X-ray time.

We found a ride to the local hospital and did *not* follow the signs to the "Casualty" wing. (I don't want to know what happens in that part of the hospital.) We signed in as new patients with minimal confusion (my file says Ryan Josephy—a creative blend of my middle and last names). The hospital was nice—clean floors, painted walls, working lights. Lots of people were waiting everywhere and wandering around places you'd think should be off limits, but nice. One of the best in Kenya I'm told. Our visit went by pretty quickly, and there were no broken bones. The only ankle braces they had were XXL, so I left empty handed, unless you want to count the small bag of Ibuprofen.

The pain in my foot persisted, which brought me to a new theory. Back in the States I had a chronic condition called neuroma which would flare up every now and then. Basically, it's a nerve between the bones in your foot that can get enlarged and aggravated every time you step. The pain felt the same as when I had a neuroma flare-up, only ten times worse. This time I could bare no weight on the foot at all.

I made some calls around campus and got in touch with the school's physical therapist. I told her my theory and my past treatment, and she looked in her box of wonders. Lo and behold—a met pad, the answer to my prayers! The met pad stuck to the insole of my shoe and relieved pressure from the metatarsal pads of my foot. No pain! I went in on crutches, discouraged and frustrated, and I left walking!

On that walk home (ironically the same walk of shame when I hurt it the week before) I felt like a king. Everyone on campus knew of my ailment, so I looked around for people to brag to. *Hey look at me...walking...* I passed someone on the stairs and used the word "miracle." She got a little uncomfortable, because she saw me on crutches the day before and now...? I had to convince Heather that it was really healed before she let me do chores that afternoon. It was actually a joy to be mobile again, working and productive. I was dancing a little gimp dance, and I don't even dance.

Now I don't really equate my situation with a miracle. My neuroma is still flaring, and the ankle is still sore. But as I was walking home, carrying my crutches, suddenly able to walk again, I thought immediately of the many people Jesus healed.

It's hard to imagine those miracles. The Bible doesn't have an Oprah-like interview with the healees about their experience. Just think though, being blind from birth and then seeing? Crippled and carried around on a mat? Bleeding from the brain...your whole life? You didn't wake up that morning with "get healed" scribbled on your dayplanner. You woke up discouraged and limited, just like any other day. Then, like a flash from heaven, you see Jesus and hear he has what you've been dying for inside. Hope. The encounter. The healing. The world is now completely different for you.

Sure, it was just a foot, and it was only a week of immobility, but I don't care. The way I feel right now, the elation, is indescribable. I'm giddy. Simply giddy.

*august 25—will work for free

The start of a new school year is just days away. They've been teaching the rookies the ropes for the past week, and we've learned one lesson very well—everything here gets charged to your account. It's become a running joke because, well, I guess it's better to laugh than to cry.

From the firewood to electricity to photocopies, you pay to work at RVA. It's an interesting place in that way. The school does have its own budget, but it's miniscule when compared to a school its size in the states. The main way it can function is by having a completely volunteer staff—dorm parents, teachers, administrators, facilities managers—all volunteers. Missionaries can't afford to send their kids to a private boarding school in Africa, so we work for free.

This creates much misunderstanding in the surrounding community, as the locals see us as the rich wazungu. The local tax authorities smell blood when they size up RVA, and they've come in for the kill especially hard these past few years. Each time it takes hours of explanation: "No, we don't pay our employees. They make no income from us. They pay to work here." You've got to be kidding, they say.

Last year, a light bulb went on for one collector. "So you mean, if a supporter promises one of your people $50 per month, and they don't give it for a few months, your worker might not be able to stay here." That's right. He gasped and exclaimed, "That is a hard life!" After that epiphany, he backed off and even begged the superintendent not to allow future tax collectors to deter us from the good work we're doing.

Each staff here gets no compensation for extra-curricular or other responsibilities which he or she takes on. The school has no leverage to make us do anything, but we give our all to provide nourishment and education for these kids. From a material point of view, we get little (sometimes less than little if supporters neglect to give) for doing a lot.

I have to admit though, being without a paycheck has really changed my attitude towards my work. I worked hard at Grossmont High School, I prayed for my students and fellow staff members, and I gave a lot of myself there. There were days, however, when I went to work for the paycheck. My eyes were on the 30th of the month rather than the mission God gave me for that day, and I think this diminished my overall impact there. On a personal level, I think that I would have found my job even more rewarding had I been able to have pure motives towards my work.

I am pouring myself into my work here already. Others do more, I know, but I'm giving more for less material gain than ever before, and…(I bet you know what I'm going to say next)…it's the most rewarding thing I've ever experienced.

Why does God set the system up like this? Why is it that the emptiest vessels are filled to the brim, those who are the most selfless find themselves filled with the most joy? Why are some enabled to take their eyes off themselves and see more glory than anyone else? His system makes me want to give more, to be emptied, to be less selfish.

And here's the kicker: those are only the rewards for us on this side. Jesus talked until He was blue in the face about heaven and the rewards for those who give and die to themselves and are cheated and love selflessly. I give everything I have, lose everything I have, and then He gives me more than I could ever imagine, more than I deserve.

God sure doesn't play fair.

*august 31—day one

One day down and 179 to go! Our first day at RVA was great. It's very odd for Heather and me to be teaching in adjacent classrooms, not to mention the same school. Not only that, but we both teach 10th grade (English and World History) so we have the same students. We've been comparing notes about them tonight, so they won't know what hit them tomorrow.

It's also odd to live with the same students you teach— we see them after school, at dinner, in their dorms, around campus. We feel like we know everybody, and the kids have only been here a few days. All in all, our start was great. We're so grateful to be *doing* what we've been *called* to do and what we've been *made* to do and what we've been *preparing* to do. As you can tell, we're excited to be here.

We found out that the information we received about our container and our e-permits was a false alarm. It turns out that AIM headquarters in New York shipped *two* containers to Kenya. Ours still hasn't arrived. So, we still have time until our e-permits come in. If this is confusing you, welcome to the club.

Hakuna matata. And yes, they really do say that here.

*september 2—rva fun facts

I really didn't know much about RVA before we got here, and I really didn't care. It was a school for MKs (missionary kids), it was in Africa, and it was big for a school of its type. That was all I really knew. I have a passion for the kids and for reaching the lost, but I didn't expect to have a passion for this school, its history, and its place in God's plan for Africa, at least not in my first weeks.

I already have pride in this place, the people who work here, and the work they are doing. Let me give you some reasons why:

- RVA is the largest boarding school in the world. Faith Academy in Manila is the largest MK school (few boarders), and Black Forest Academy in Germany is second largest with boarders. So, who cares? Running a boarding school takes immense staffing, infrastructure,

and funding. As I stated before, we run on faith here—
tuition is low, staffing is free, and everything else is
donated. And it's been like this for 100 years.

- RVA has a stellar reputation throughout the world. We
  were the first school in Africa to receive accreditation by
  the United States (1968), and our graduates pepper
  white-collar professions worldwide. Recently, RVA
  grads have been accepted at Harvard, Yale, Princeton,
  Stanford, Duke, Cornell, and Dartmouth; one former
  student is currently a Rhodes Scholar. Harvard recently
  ranked RVA as the top American college preparatory
  school in Africa, with a nonreligious swanky school in
  South Africa behind us.
- RVA's student body is one of a kind. Students come
  from 21 different home countries (the U.S. leads with
  57% of the student body and South Korea is in second
  with 14%), and their parents are working in 21 different
  countries. In my 10th and 8th grade English classes
  alone, there are 13 different nationalities represented.
  Students speak multiple languages, have traveled alone
  internationally, and have lived in the middle of
  devastating circumstances like genocide.

Size, excellence, diversity—three understatements when it
comes to describing this school. By the grace of God (another
understatement), RVA presses on into its second century.

*september 9—lunch with a multi-millionaire

"Prior to the year A.D. 1000, the most productive areas
of the world were two to three times more prosperous than the
poorer areas. Europe and Africa were on an approximately
equal level economically. The situation began to change
dramatically with the Industrial Revolution. Today the ratio is
about sixty to one, and the economic gap continues to widen
dramatically. This means that the average Westerner will have
access to sixty times more wealth in a lifetime than will the
average African" (*African Friends and Money Matters*, p. 201).

I had lunch the other day with someone whom I was 60 times more wealthy than. Martha invited us to her home, where she and her three daughters live. She lives in one of four units, which, in total size, is much smaller than my parents' garage. Her individual unit was the size of our apartment's bedroom. Two hanging curtains separated the back part where the women slept from the front half, where the seven of us sat, ate, and visited.

They had a small camping cooker on the top shelf which they cooked on when the weather was bad. On this sunny day, they cooked the vegetables over a charcoal pit. We were served beans, potatoes, and peas mashed together (a dish called irio), and it was quite good. However, that and ugali—a maize dish—are all our hosts ever eat. (Our common question "What do you feel like eating tonight?" is quite nonsensical here.)

They walk to a nearby well for their water, and they share an outhouse with the three other families. Electricity is one of their few luxuries, and that enables them to listen to their Christian music tapes on a small stereo. Their door has a lock on it because, even though they have next to nothing, there are others who are less fortunate or are more greedy. These were some things I noticed during the meal.

After we ate, Micah went outside and played with the nine children who belonged to the neighbors (half a dozen more were away on this day). They laughed at our little ghost and touched his hair that was as silky and blond as the corn husks that they played among.

We stayed inside and heard of Martha's struggle to put her two eldest daughters through high school (grades 1-8 are free in Kenya; students have to pay for high school) and to take care of her two year old. There is more to her remarkable story than I have room to tell right now.

After visiting with Martha for a while, the daughters walked us to the nearby airstrip perched on the edge of the mountain. Planes will only use this in case of emergency because the winds coming off the valley floor are so blustery.

One time two planes in a row crashed on the same day. I doubt people in Kijabe hear "flying is safer than driving" very often. Or at least not without laughing.

They said the walk wasn't far, but we quickly learned that the American definition of far was different than theirs. Tabitha, the eldest, has dreams of attending college in the United States. She's second in her class at a very good girls' school and asked us what tuition costs. I explained sadly that the cheapest universities in the States cost about the equivalent of 800 years worth of wages for the average Kenyan, and she couldn't even fathom what expensive schools cost.

Four hours after we arrived, we began the walk home, through the corn fields and the sheep herds, past the shacks and the open sewers. Back up the mountain to our little American school oasis.

I can't say I know what it feels like in the reverse. I don't hang out with many multi-millionaires back in the States. And there's probably a reason that it rarely happens. It's uncomfortable.

This is the discomfort that's become a way of life here, and I have to think that if I ever do become comfortable with it, there is something seriously wrong with me.

*september 21—the adrenaline buzz

According to our calendars, it's the first day of fall today. As things are probably starting to cool off back home, the days are getting warmer and drier here south of the equator. It's still windy as all get out, but it's warming up. Time to start putting sunscreen on our white little boy. His semi-albino father should use some too.

I read this verse in my Bible today. *Keep your eyes on Jesus, who both began and finished this race we're in. Study how he did it. Because he never lost sight of where he was headed--that exhilarating finish in and with God—he could put up with anything along the way: cross, shame, whatever. (Hebrews 12:2-3 The Message)*

Just like in a race, we started out this school year on pure adrenaline, excited to be underway and looking forward to seeing how this amazing school operates. Now, we've come to the point where the adrenaline wears off, we're breathing heavily, and we've only come around the first turn. Things are intense here. It's a big school with lots of needs, and teaching is just one of our jobs. We're practicing the art of *no*, but somehow we still have this secret affection for *yes*.

Heather's pretty beat up. She's teaching and helping out with the high school worship band and managing our family life at the same time. All that plus she's been constantly sick—a rash, then a fever, then stomach problems, and now a head cold. But, it's okay really. God's Spirit is pumping through our veins and will see us to the end.

The honeymoon is over for the dorm parents and for the teachers too. The kids here are great; don't get me wrong. But they're still kids, and they share in that common characteristic we all have as fallen human beings. Conflicts abound, different kids are getting suspended and disciplined every day, but hopefully there is forgiveness somewhere in all of this, too. There's no other way for us to survive unless we live for forgiveness.

*september 26—pronounced "em-kay"

If you haven't learned my abbreviations yet, MK stands for missionary kid. Thousands of MKs exist worldwide, having grown up in millions of remote and exotic settings, and they all share some common traits. There is a humorous book called *You Know You're an MK When...* that compiled some of their similarities. I stole some of my favorites from there.

10. You can't answer the question, "Where are you from?"

9. You have a trunk for a coffee table.

8. The vast majority of your clothes are hand-me downs.

7. You flew before you could walk.

6. The U.S. is a foreign country.
5. You have a passport, but no driver's license.
4. You watch *National Geographic* specials and recognize someone.
3. You consider a city 500 miles away to be "very close".
2. You believe vehemently that football is played with a round spotted ball.
1. You'd rather never say hello than have to say goodbye.

It's crazy to think that I've done this to my son. What kind of life is he going to lead? It's going to be a tad different than growing up in little Red Lion, Pennsylvania. He'll love it (I think); this place has so much freedom and adventure to offer a kid. But he'll have a whole set of problems and frustrations that I never had.

*september 28—soil and sacrifice

For the past year or so, folks have been asking me, in effect, "Isn't it going to be hard to leave everything behind?" I guess my response was pretty tepid all along. It wasn't that I didn't think there was any sacrifice involved. It wasn't that I thought it wasn't a big deal—to leave your family, friends, country, culture. Maybe it was just too big of a deal, too big to understand, to digest, and to feel.

Well, three months into this thing I'm beginning to feel. Pictures from our goodbye parties, souvenirs from our last outings with family, emails from supporters, and the occasional brief phone call—all bittersweet tastes of home.

It's only when you miss something and when it hurts that it really becomes a sacrifice. Otherwise, it's a change or an adjustment or a self-serving choice. It's not a sacrifice until you feel it.

Sacrifice is a sign of love. You give up something for someone else. You put that person ahead of yourself. God could not have sacrificed more than He did by becoming human and going to the cross. I'm only following His lead.

I'm telling God that I love Him more than I love anything in the world when my heart hurts. I won't turn around or give up His call because it hurts a lot. I'll just give it to Him as a humble gift, as an offering. King David said, "I will not...sacrifice a burnt offering that costs me nothing."

Over and over, God tells us that He really starts to work when we hurt for Him, when we want what He wants more than anything. And that's where I am and that's why I know He's about to get to work. There is excitement in this pain, therefore, because the Creator of the universe is about to sit down at the piano and make Mozart look like a monkey. My life will be His score. This I believe.

To put it in terms that my Kenyan neighbors could relate to—sacrifice is the soil of True Life, and the darker and richer it is, the greater the harvest.

*september 29—this week's top two

We got some big news this week.

The Kuiper family (Heather's side) welcomed into the world Christian Thomas Kuiper on Tuesday. We were so lucky to be able to talk with them on the phone after the delivery and see a few pictures via email. They didn't even look like they hadn't slept in 30 hours! Momma Cathy and Daddy Jason are as proud as can be, and our Micah can't wait to wrestle with his new cousin.

The second most exciting news for this week has been the arrival of our container! We got a call on Thursday saying that we needed to pick up our stuff immediately because it was taking up space at the Nairobi office. Talk about anticlimactic.

Luckily, an RVA van was in town on Thursday and an RVA truck went to town on Friday. They were able to bring home about 75% of our shipment. Hopefully the remaining 25% will make it here early next week. There are a few things broken so far, which is quite amazing considering some of the cardboard boxes look like they'd been run over by a rhino.

We haven't heard what the "damage" is yet pertaining to our customs fees, and we don't want to know right now. We're just enjoying unpacking and praising God for its arrival half way around the world. Heather made a cake tonight with good old Betty Crocker mix, and my guitar has never sounded sweeter.

*october 1—rich poor man

So I just went on and on about how great it was to receive our shipment from the States. Material goods, creature comforts, all are ours—thanks to our successful careers in America and the generosity of supporters. But now I'm going to try to tell you that I'm a poor man.

I used to own a house, but we sold it to get out of debt and to get to the mission field. I don't have a job that pays me a salary. I support my family from the money that other people and churches have given to us. I'll pay almost nothing in taxes this year because in the States we live far below the poverty line.

Missionaries are not wealthy people by American standards. Sure, some of us may have retirement accounts and assets (savings, stocks, property, etc.), but when you consider disposable income and the ability to grow financially, we're quite impotent. Remove us from the States though, and place us just about anywhere else in the world, and we somehow rise to the top of the wealth chart. Within a five mile radius from where I sit right now, I'm one of richest men in sight.

I'm a rich man. How can this be? The average Kenyan earns a dollar a day. A married couple can rake in $60 a month. Is this even enough to survive, you may ask? Yes and no. For normal living it's enough. Throw in any kind of emergency to the equation, and their salary will be found lacking. This would concern us in the States—not having enough money for school fees or delivering a baby or (eh hem) a broken foot. Their culture, however, has ways of providing for such situations.

If you were a Kenyan, you'd simply ask your neighbors and relatives for the money that you were in need of. Yes, they are the same people that only make $60/mo. themselves, but everybody has a few dollars lying around. In the States, we'd say, "I can't give you five dollars because I need to buy food next week." A foreign concept here. The immediate need gives way to a future need always. You give the $5 and figure out later how you'll buy food.

You borrow money on credit here, but not from an impersonal institution like Visa or American Express. Your credit is with your relationships. You literally invest in the lives of those you love by helping them out with needs that are too big for them. Paying back money isn't usually the norm, either. You are still in debt, but the opportunity to return the favor will surface in some other way. Perhaps next month your cousin will need money for a wedding ceremony (people get in over their heads here even more than in the States when they marry); you will contribute something when they ask, to be sure.

Having this in mind, picture me. I'm typing away on a laptop computer (which someone bought for us) while eating my breakfast, which I made from among a two-week supply of food in our refrigerator (also a gift from supporters). I have a few thousand shillings in my wallet (about $30) that I won't spend today or even tomorrow, but that I will need sometime in the next few days.

Am I rich by American standards as I sit here? Far from it. I may be equipped and suitably supplied, but everything I own has been given to me. I have little liquid funds. I'm ill-prepared for any urgent emergency, and I'm not self-sufficient to provide for my family. Without supporters, I'd start the long walk home (and swim?) tomorrow.

In a Kenyan's eyes, am I rich? If I have the credit (i.e. relationships) to own a laptop computer, a refrigerator, and have $30 in my wallet, then I am rich. Period.

And when someone here knocks on my door and asks me for a few thousand shillings because he needs to pay for his child's hospital bill, what will I say? I don't have the money? Go ask someone in your family? I am not a rich man? How I answer will determine the kind of ministry I will have here. Because relationships are credit, and your credit is your relationships.

*october 6—the wounded and the sick

This week is Spiritual Emphasis Week on campus. We have a guest speaker coming from the States, and he'll be speaking on "The Wounded Healer." I've seen his outline, and he's really going to be getting to the hearts of a lot of kids. He'll be talking about our hurts and the uncertainty of the future and how God can heal us of all our wounds. As a school body, we've had a rough start to the year. Six seniors have been suspended (two of which will probably be expelled) for bringing alcohol to campus and getting drunk. This has led to some animosity between the guilty parties, their friends, and the administration that disciplined them. We are in need of healing and a fresh passion for God as a school. Heather and I will be leading worship for all of the sessions (five nights, Wednesday through Sunday) and for Sunday morning's worship time.

I missed school today with a fever of 101, and Heather is having stomach problems today. It probably sounds like we're sick all the time over here. We're not always sick, but we've had more than a normal amount of illness since we've been here. I think I was sick once all of last year, and I'm already on #3 this term.

*october 8—one man's trash is another cow's lunch

There was a time in high school when I was very environmentally conscious. I stopped flushing the toilet, started saving aluminum, and eliminated all meat-eating from my diet. It was hard work, going against the grain of your family, your culture, and your own conditioning. Over time, I relaxed.

Now I wouldn't go so far as to call myself a gasoline-drinking, leather-wearing, endangered-species-eating, landfill-abusing monster, but I wasn't a Sierra Club poster boy either. I am an American. I had a 100 gallon trash can provided for me by the City of San Diego, and I filled it frequently. I am an American. We waste. It's increasingly an American characteristic.

You won't find 100 gallon receptacles here. The paper goods (and plastic and just about every other material, sadly) which make their way into a Kenyan's hands ultimately find the burn pile. The pervasive smell of smoke overwhelmed us initially—on the side of the roads, outside of the houses, in front of businesses—but we've grown more accustomed. We've adjusted in more ways than one to this trashless yet trash-impacted society.

Since we're temporary Kenyans, we don't have one big trashcan like we used to; we organize it in different ways now. Our living room's "firewood" pile looks extremely trashy. While you'll find sticks and logs in it, we also have an accumulation of old mail, school papers, and cardboard. It's not trash; it's a fuel source.

Another place that looks trashy is the area around our kitchen sink. Rather than throw away old cans, bottles, and containers, we wash them out and give them out in the community. Jars serve as Tupperware for locals to keep food in, plastic bottles second as drink containers, and tin cans double as sauce pans to cook in. Recycling. Third World style.

Under the sink, we have a "food scraps" container with a lid on it. What used to go down our garbage disposal now gets bagged up twice a week and goes home with our nanny, Susan. Being typical Kenyans, Susan and her husband have various animals at home—the chief one being a cow. Fairly nutritious items frequently go uneaten during our meals; rather than becoming trash, leftovers become sustenance for their sources of sustenance. (I can hear Elton John singing "The Circle of Life" in the background.)

Lastly, you may be able to take the boy out of America, but you can't take America completely out of the boy. We do still have a good old red-white-and-blue trashcan. But at its 3 gallon size, it's a far cry from our 100 gallon jobbie in the USA.

Trash was just a compartmentalized part of our old lives. Water, fuel, sewage, food, trash—each one its place, each used without regard for the other, each frequently abused. But there are no dividing lines here, and it's honestly easier to respect our resources. I'm learning not to waste my trash; it's usable.

*october 16—"My grace is sufficient"

Here's the overview of the happenings during Spiritual Emphasis Week. I was sick, sick, sick last Monday and Tuesday, and then Tuesday night (when we had a very important music practice scheduled) I began feeling better. The practice went well, and I was back at school on Wednesday. This was obviously a gift from God. I'm not sure what would've happened if I were sick for another day or two.

The first night was rough musically, but Thursday night was incredible—both the worship and the speaker. After he spoke on sexual purity and healing, there was an extended prayer time for kids who needed it and the worship team played until 10 p.m. Poor Micah stayed awake the entire time and was a real trooper, but this night really got him off of his schedule.

On Friday night, the students were challenged on this night to make amends with others. As we played for the last 30 minutes, kids were walking around, talking and hugging, sitting together and praying. Very unique. I'd never been a part of this kind of thing, but it's so Biblically sound. Jesus told us to do this every time we bring an offering to God! Reconciliation is more important to God than a lot of other things that we often put first.

That night Micah didn't sleep much, which was very uncharacteristic for him. We were exhausted the next day, but we still had three more times to lead—Saturday night, Sunday morning, and Sunday evening. We prayed prayers of desperation before bed Saturday night. The kinds with a bunch of tears accompanying them. We were run ragged and spiritually empty.

God heard our cries. We woke up with energy on Sunday morning and led the 600+ church service very well. The students felt very comfortable with us and the older folks did too. And Sunday night's session was a great conclusion. There was a 45 minute altar call (during which the worship team played again) and a dozen kids decided to follow Jesus for the first time in their lives. Dozens more came up for prayer, and there was a bonfire and testimony time after the service.

Of course it's hard to measure anything spiritual. Numbers don't really do it. In fact, we'll never be able to know the impact of the worship and the messages and the times of prayer. We trust that God has moved in this time that we set aside for Him to move, and we pray for it to continue here in "unscheduled" times.

As for us, we're still recovering at this point although school has been very busy this week. We're very grateful for God's power to persevere and for a "mission accomplished."

*october 18—checklist for home

In the tradition of the book *You Know You're an MK When...*, some clever RVA staff came up with our own. This is a weird little African and yet Western place, and its peculiarities are hard to digest at first. I'll explain them in more detail later, but for now, you know RVA is home when...

10. Your white sneakers are the same color as everyone else's.

9. You know what all the keys on your key ring are for.

8. You figure out how to flush your own toilet.

7. You are territorial about your seat during chai time.

6. You are able to finish your chai before 4th period.

5. You learn to save your computer work every five minutes.

4. You remember to take toilet paper with you every time you leave campus.
3. You can still breathe when you get to the top of the hill.
2. You've learned how to grunt "hello" in three different languages.
1. The whole campus knows whether you wear boxers or briefs.

*october 20—through different eyes

Something unusual has happened to me—the Bible has come alive. Growing up in the American church, the Bible specifically and faith in general always had a foreign feel to them. The only time we ever wore robes and held staffs in my hometown was during the Easter pageants. Nobody rode donkeys or chariots in Red Lion, and good luck trying to find a Roman centurion at the local police station. Somehow church teachings felt like somebody else's shoes I was trying to make fit.

Once I became a Christian at 18, I saw for the first time how God fit into my culture and my real life. My Bible reading exploded, and I saw everything with new eyes. I studied it like crazy and miraculously grew in spiritual and emotional ways. I think I had an adequate understanding of Scriptures, in the light of the culture in which I read the words, but now, being here has opened up a whole new cultural relevance that I couldn't experience previously. I'll give you few samples.

• Everyone walks here, and not just to their cars or for exercise, like in the States. They walk to church, to work, to visit friends, and to most anywhere they need to go. I can picture the towns of Jesus' day because I've seen the crowds walking along the roads, swarming the cities, and dotting the farm lands. It's a slower pace of life, so there is more time for relationships and conversation. Oral cultures, like that of Old Testament times, thrive on word of mouth and on time taken to listen. If something happens here in

Kijabe, people know about it in Limuru within a few hours. When Jesus walked the Earth, word spread quickly, not by an impersonal newspaper or evening news but by a personal friend who spent time walking with Him.

- The elders have extreme power in most towns and villages. Your reputation and even your livelihood are in their hands. Yes, that's the kind of power they have—the power to grant you or to keep you from a job. Ever tried to pay for food or shelter or clothes without a job? Some wield their power in godly ways and some selfishly, but this is the system. I can now imagine the threat that Jesus posed to the establishment. He usurped the existing power structure of the society, and the fear the Jews felt was not just for their religion's survival or their people's safety versus the Romans, but for their culture's very foundation itself.

- Connected to the power of elders is the idea of complete authority. Kenya's government is a democracy, but in matters of daily living, there are many situations where life is beyond an individual's control. Someone else has the authority—whether it be an elder or a chief or an armed rebel or the police officer who stops you. It's complete control, beyond fairness or "the law" many times. In the States, you commit a crime against me, I call the police. If the policeman isn't just, I go above him. If the department isn't just, I sue. Heck, I'm even allowed to sport on my bumper a slogan that says "Not my president" about the most powerful man in the land. When the Bible talks about a king or a wealthy land owner, Americans can't fully understand all of the authority that those positions entail. We may sing, "Jesus, You are my king," but we actually mean, "Jesus, You are my current employer whom I will respect and work for as long as it is advantageous to me in my present locale." Kingship is a lost metaphor.

I could go on, from women's roles to marriage customs to the importance of livestock. There is so much here that helps me understand the Bible. I'm not saying Kenya is thousands of years behind the West, stuck in Abraham's day. Kenya is changing, as are all cultures, but what they have in common with the Middle Eastern cultures of the Bible is far more abundant than what my home culture does.

*october 26—whiny boy

Okay, so my wife and I don't share all of the same musical tastes. One of my favorite song writers is Derek Webb (formerly of the band Caedmon's Call). Heather bristles every time she hears him and has affectionately labeled him "Whiny Boy." I love his style though. With a little guitar, a little piano, and (yes, I'll confess) a little whine, he hits right between the eyes. He says in his songs for all to hear what you think in your head when you think God might not be listening.

The song of his that's really rocking my roost right now is called "I repent." Its topic, fittingly, is repentance, which is a rare and lost art these days, in my opinion. It seems like when somebody does actually repent, it's never about anything that really needs repenting of to begin with. Kind of keeps the church of Jesus Christ impotent if all the sinners never even admit to ever sinning.

Anyway, this is off his album *I see things upside down.* Read it in your whiniest head voice, all right?

I repent, I repent
Of my pursuit of America's dream
Of living like I deserve anything
Of my house, my fence, my kids, my wife
In our suburb where we're safe and white
Oh, I am wrong and of these things I repent

I repent, I repent
Of parading my high liberty
Of paying for what I get for free
For the way I believe that I'm living right

By trading sins for others that are easier to hide
Oh, I am wrong and of these things I repent

I repent, I repent
Of trading truth for false unity
Of confusing peace and idolatry
By caring more of what they think than what I know of what we
need
Of domesticating You until You look just like me
Oh, I am wrong and of these things I repent

*october 29—battling violent monkeys

A few folks have asked us what a typical day is like for us. Do we commute on an elephant, do we kill our own goats, do we bathe regularly? You know, questions like that. I hope this helps connect the dots.

6 a.m. Dorm girls upstairs wake up and roosters begin to crow, so naturally, we wake up. We have some time with God to start our day, eat some breakfast, and yes, we do bathe.

7:45 Ryan's first class—sophomore English. Ryan's three high school classes are all before chapel. Heather and Micah are dressing and eating breakfast.

8:15 Heather walks Micah ¼ mile uphill to our friend Joan's house. Their dog is truly Micah's favorite babysitter.

8:30 Heather's one high school morning class.

10:15 Chapel. A teacher or a dorm parent brings a short message from the Bible. Joan brings Micah to chapel, and then Heather watches him for the rest of the morning.

10:30 Chai break. This British custom has been whole-heartedly adopted by Kenyans. A Kenyan doctor in the middle of surgery will leave the patient on the table for chai break.

10:45 Ryan's first eighth grade English class.

11:30 Ryan's guitar class for beginners.

12:30 p.m. Heather and Micah meet Ryan in the cafo (RVA's nickname for the cafeteria) for lunch. This is our equivalent of "eating out." Micah likes visiting all 25 tables of students as soon as he finishes eating.

1:00 Micah's nanny Susan arrives and puts him down for his nap. We go to school to grade papers and lesson plan.

1:45 Heather's two afternoon World History classes. Ryan's second eighth grade class and then a seventh grade study hall with a bunch of spastic angels.

3:30 Eighth period begins, which is time for extra study help and make-up exams. We speak to the custodians in Kikuyu, and they laugh.

4:30 The school day is over. We head home and relieve our nanny. Our language helper, Priscilla, arrives and helps us with out Kikuyu for an hour.

6:00 Dinner. Usually something quick and easy, like spaghetti or burgers. We've eaten more hot dogs in the past 4 months of marriage than in the previous 5 years combined.

7:00 Heather helps out with the high school worship band. Ryan and Micah have some male-bonding time, which consists of wrestling, reading truck books, and watching Veggie Tales.

8:45 Micah's bedtime. He gives Mama a hug and hears his personal lullabye from Dad. He's out for the night.

9:00 Ryan and Heather prepare lessons for the next day and send off a few emails to friends and family.

10:30 Dorm girls upstairs stop making noise so we can now go to sleep. We pray and then pass out.

So there you have it. The cold hard facts. No rhinoceros rides or battles with violent monkeys. Just a busy day teaching and helping out here at RVA, learning the language and culture, taking in each experience one at a time. Eating our elephant nice and slowly.

FOUR

homeless for the holidays

NOVEMBER 2005- JANUARY 2006

We want to introduce you to a new member of our family. No, we're not expecting another child, and I'm not talking about our new kitten. You need to meet Susan, our nanny and house helper.

Susan Nduta is a Kikuyu woman who is a few weeks older than Heather (for the sake of my health, I'll refrain from announcing exactly how old that is). She's married to Biden, and they have three children: Kristin, 10; Hannah, 8; and Brian, 4. They live two miles from RVA's campus (uphill), and they usually walk to work (rain or shine) together since Biden is a groundskeeper here.

Both were unemployed for the past year, and this was hard on their family. Now that Susan is working for us and Biden also is working for a long-term missionary family, their situation has improved dramatically. They've been able to buy the land on which they've been living and also a sheep. (Buying a sheep is kind of like buying stocks here, just a bit messier.) The view they have from their front door would make you envious—a 120 degree view of the Great Rift Valley from a wooded hillside.

Their home is a three room, 400 square feet unit with an outhouse outside. They have a cow and a four month old calf, in addition to their new sheep. They have a shamba (large garden) which grows various crops with corn being the staple. Susan's "kitchen" is a small shed outside their home where they can build a fire to cook over or use small propane burners.

Selling tortillas and English muffins at the RVA market once a week brings in a little extra income to her family.

Susan watches Micah every day for us. Susan also helps us around the house with cleaning, cooking, and laundry when Micah doesn't need her constant attention. She's speaks to him in Kikuyu all day so he's learning two languages right now. He walks all over campus with her, and more Kenyans know him than know us. When I walk around with him, most people greet Micah and know me only as Baba Micah (father of Micah). I don't mind being second fiddle.

We are so glad that God brought Susan into our lives. Our hope is that she'd be our friend and worker for all of our years here, that we'd have a lifelong relationship that would be mutually beneficial and honor the Lord.

*november 4—house workers

My first experience with house workers was back in 2000. I awoke in the morning to the sound of Donna, a missionary from my church in San Diego whom I was visiting, and two Filipina ladies in the kitchen on my first short mission trip. Donna, her husband, and I were the only ones in the house when we went to sleep the night before, so I wondered what the other voices were. I didn't know Bill and Donna had house workers.

House workers? I thought missionaries were supposed to be rugged and hard-working and all of that. The only people that have people working for them in the States are the very rich, the very busy, or business owners. My ideal image of the "missionary life" was being shattered. What was going on here?

This is a complex issue, I've learned, but one that's changed from being distasteful to beautiful in my opinion. I've outlined briefly how different the financial worlds are for us in Africa, and this is another prime illustration.

When we came to this school, the Kenyan community understood perfectly why we came, where we came from, and how much money we must have to be here. Thus, there was another expectation placed on us—to share our wealth by employing a local person. Not to meet this expectation would be to hurt their community, to display selfishness, and to show a lack of sensitivity to the culture and needs around us. If we had thought about not employing a worker (which we had) before we came here, it was severely discouraged by the experienced missionaries at RVA, especially for folks like us who want to make inroads in the local culture and make a career of teaching here.

The minimum wage here is atrocious by States' standards. Hire a nanny or a cleaning lady in America, and it'll set you back at least $10 an hour. Probably much, much more. We don't set the minimum wage here; it's set by the economy and the standards set for employment by Kenyans. The employment rate (not unemployment rate, *employment*) is at around 30%, so workers aren't scarce and thousands are hungry for a paycheck. The going rate for basic labor is somewhere between 50 cents and $1.50 an hour.

Before you throw down your book in outrage and label me another Kathie Lee Gifford, let me explain further. We can't pay our workers more, can't pay them a "fair rate" according to our home cultures without disrupting the local community. If I chose to pay our worker $15 an hour for working for us, her life would change drastically for the worse.

How? First off, her relatives would probably all quit working. With Susan making enough for all of them to live off of, why should they work? You might be saying, *Wait, that's her money. Not theirs.* True, from a Westerner's point of view. In an African's eyes, you have access to any windfall that comes to a relative, friend, or even a neighbor. To be a good sister, daughter, friend, neighbor, etc., Susan would have to share. She'd have no choice.

Secondly, she'd have to move out of the area. The improvements she could make to her house, her property, and her wardrobe would be substantial, but they'd also cause her to stick out like a sore thumb. She'd be a target for theft, vandalism, and possibly violence. The nail that sticks out gets hammered down in Kenyan culture.

Thirdly, other workers in the community would be outraged. *Why should she get rich for doing the same work we're doing?* They'd be angry with their employers, with us, and with Susan. Fourthly, it would damage the balance of the Kenyan economy. Even if I could afford to pay her $15 an hour (which I can't), Kenyans who need to hire basic labor can't. If they have to raise their wages to even twice what they are that would have devastating effects on the economy. (Kind of like the labor unions in the States wanting more and more money as they watch the manual labor jobs move overseas.)

Do you see how complex this is? You could say that we are choosing to have a worker and to pay them low wages. Or you could say that the society and our position in this society as Westerners dictate these choices. I'll admit, it feels strange, but as I'll point out later, the blessings of this work relationship are enormous for everyone involved.

*november 7—election times

This email was sent yesterday from RVA's superintendent Tim Cook to parents and staff of the school.

"As many of you are aware, Kenya has been undergoing a constitutional review process for a number of years. A new constitution has been proposed and there is strong debate throughout the country. Many of the rallies for or against the proposed constitution have been accompanied by violence. After consultation with other AIM leaders in Kenya, the RVA administration made a decision to move leaving day up to the 19th of November. This decision was made out of concern for the potential disruption to travel because of the referendum during the week of the 21st of November. *The school does NOT feel any danger here at Kijabe...*However, parents would have to travel through urban centers to reach RVA and it is in these centers that trouble may happen. So as a precautionary measure,

RVA has decided to close early. We covet your prayers for a peaceful referendum process."

You should have heard the cheer that went up from the kids when they announced this on Friday. Finals were supposed to begin on November 18th but they've been cancelled because of the early leaving date. (You won't hear too many teachers complaining about not having to grade the tests either) Kijabe is about an hour outside of Nairobi so, like Tim said, we should be very safe here. Regardless, we're praying for a peaceful election and transition to the new constitution. Peace in this country has far reaching, positive effects on the gospel going out to the places where our students' parents work.

*november 16—i bless the rains down in africa

I doubt Susan (or anybody in Kijabe for that matter) has ever heard of the rock band Toto. But if she had, I know she'd love them. How can you *not* love Toto? Come on, 80's music buffs…sing along. I know you want to.

"It's gonna take a lot to get me away from you/There's nothing that a hundred men or more could ever do/ I bless the rains down in Africa/Gonna take some time to do the things we never have."

I have no idea what they were talking about in that song, but, nevertheless, I find it running through my head quite frequently. I guess it's because I'm always thinking about rain these days. The lack of rain is a storied part of the history of this continent, and another area of lifestyle adjustment for us has been water.

We don't live in an arid part of Africa. People often "ooh" and "ahh" about the fact that we have grass here most of the year. And it's green! We live on the side of a mountain that overlooks the Great Rift Valley, and we get quite a bit of rain. The valley floor is brown and dry much of the year, but our hill is filled with trees and greenery. Still, lack of water is always a concern.

It's the beginning of the "dry season" here, and we just ended a strict water conservation spell. Our well pumps had been working overtime during about a month of dry weather until we had two straight days of rain last weekend. To let you know what kind of a water need we have as a school campus, I'll remind you that there are about 100 adults and 500 kids here. We have a sewer system that runs on gravity, so it takes a ton of water to flush all of your waste through. There is a laundry facility that washes students' clothes all week long. The long and short of it—we need and use lots of water.

As a family, we take every measure to conserve what we can, in and out of dry season. A bucket in our bathroom and a tub in our kitchen sink catch "gray" water, and we reuse it in our toilet or for the plants outside. A hose also takes soapy and rinse cycle water from our washing machine to a small tank outside for use in the garden. Another tank sits under the rain gutters to catch rains and dews for future use. Of course, we don't keep the water running for washing dishes and take short showers (yes, even Heather).

The other aspect of water here is its drinkability (don't look it up, it's not a word, trust me). Because we're high on the mountain, our water is (with only a slight filtering process) clean. Clean water in Africa? Yes. This is a rare place. To make the water even better, they add fluoride to it which is great for all of the children here. Not for babies though. Little kids' teeth will turn yellow if they drink the tap water. Therefore, Micah can't drink the water from the tap, but for very different reasons than any other American kid in Africa—vanity not safety. Kind of ironic.

Considering how important water is, the story of how RVA ended up here in Kijabe is pretty miraculous. Charles Hurlburt, a leader of AIM around the turn of the 19th century, was scouting out places to put a mission station. He found a beautiful piece of land by Lake Naivasha, an hour northwest of Kijabe. He put a bid on it and thought he had it when Lord Delamere, a British colonist infamous for his decadence, came through and saw the land. He said it was too beautiful to be wasted on missionaries; his bid was higher and Delamere Dairy still operates there today.

Sad story? Hardly. The water table there is so low now that the school would've had to move decades ago. The water there is not drinkable, so we'd need to boil every drop that touched our mouths. Plus, that property is in a malaria zone. All staff and students would have struggled with medications and frequent bouts of malaria if the school had landed there. Not to mention that Lake Naivasha is a good 10 degrees warmer year round than Kijabe. Did God have his hand on the placement of this school? Decide for yourself.

Although we have it great here in Kijabe, we still pray for rain all the time. And the joy that we get from rain is unique. Rains mean less inconvenience for us at RVA, which is nice but no big deal. For our neighbors and friends in this community though, it means strong crops, water for drinking, and life itself. Rain is a blessing from God to Africa, but I guess it's good to have Toto's blessing too.

*november 25—a very sick little boy

Our hearts are heavy tonight. Our two month old nephew Christian, whom we've never met before, is in critical care at Children's Hospital in San Diego with two bad infections—one respiratory and the other intestinal. He's been in the hospital for days now, but we just found out today. They say he's really fighting hard.

We feel powerless and confused and so far away. We don't know what else to do but pray. Pray for his healing and the Lord's mercy on him. Pray for Jason and Cathy—his parents. Pray for grandparents and all of the other friends and family who are there by their sides.

If we were there, life would stop. We'd be at the hospital, we'd be helping taking care of our 3 year old niece Tierra, we'd be doing something.

Here we can do nothing. Life must go on as usual, normal on the outside but heavy on the inside.

Nothing is outside of God's control, and so we look to Him for answers and comfort and miracles. We will trust in Him. Trust and wait—for phone calls to come, for emails, for any news about his condition.

*november 28—i love technology

During our deputation, I did a talk for the youth group at my home church in San Diego. I love those kids so much that I wanted to do something special for them. I worked for hours on a little video clip with a hot Switchfoot song, and I was jazzed to use it as my finale. So when I was ready for it, I addressed the beautiful but shy young lady running the projector and TV screens with the highest title of respect I could think of. I said, "If the tech geek could start the video now please?"

Tech geek. You'd take that as a compliment, right?

It turns out that the boys in the youth group enjoyed this new nickname for her, and the ribbing began immediately after my inspirational message was over. Luckily, Jessica is one of my wife's best friends, and she forgave me as soon as she was sure I was out of the country.

I love tech geeks, and we recently met a whole team of tech geeks. Yes, a team of them. Tech geeks on a mission.

A guy named Shaun started a group called Missionary Tech Support with the goal of supporting full-time missionaries in remote places with their technology needs. He knew the importance of computers to translators and Bible professors and just about everybody else on the field, too, but he also knew that keeping those machines running in the middle of the jungle or a third-world country is a challenge.

Rather than traipse his team through all of the remote places though, he strategically planned to do short-term mission trips when missionaries were gathered. Most organizations will have their scattered missionaries meet about once a year in a centralized location, and that's where Shaun's teams go.

Last week, all of AIM's Kenya missionaries met here on our school's campus for a week of meetings and spiritual encouragement from Reverend Eddie from the U.K.. He spoke on resting in the Lord, which was a sorely needed topic for Heather and me as we've been worried about our nephew. We also helped with the high school program (about 50 kids) by leading worship every night of the six day conference. But while the missionaries were in meetings, Shaun's tech geeks were at work. From early in the morning until late at night, missionaries brought their poor, their sick, their lame computers unto the team and they healed them.

Well, most of them. The team had bad news for me. "You let the smoke out of your laptop," they said, which for those of you who don't speak Techgeekese means, "This computer is dead." However, they were able to retrieve my old files somehow, including e-mails which were potentially the biggest loss, and they agreed to transport my laptop back to the States with them at the end of their stay and mail it to Hewlett Packard. It's under warranty until December 31, so there's a good chance HP will fix or replace it for me for free.

1 Corinthians 12 talks about the parts of the body and how they all work together, and while Paul probably never conceived that tech geeks would one day be a part of the body of Christ, they definitely have their place. It seems obvious that tech geeks would be needed in the wealthy, advanced Western countries for their snazzy church services and outreaches, but in missions? Tech geeks aren't evangelists, translators, teachers, doctors, so how do tech geeks help reach the unreached?

By using their gifts to support others whose gifts directly touch the lost. That's the best kind of short term mission trip—the ones that encourage and strengthen the missionaries who have the relationships and the respect of the people who are lost and in need. And tech geeks definitely have skills and time and money to offer us to make our ministries more effective here in the long term.

Tech geek—a high compliment. Tech geek with a passion for the lost—a person worthy of my highest praise.

*december 3—peace on earth

It's that time of the year again. The time when many Americans focus on love and peace more than any other time, on giving rather than getting, on trying to get some perspective on their radically fast paced lives. The phrase "peace on earth" rings out from department store stereos, and ironically, just the very presence of the individual in that sterile, safe mall means peace has been achieved. We couldn't really say the same thing here in Kenya this week.

Although Kenya's been free from British rule for over half a century and has a working constitution, the ruling party decided to write a new constitution on their own. As in the U.S., political parties don't get along very well, and this slows down the process. Since this constitution wasn't a joint effort, opposition was fierce. Debates, protests, and riots have been going on sporadically over the past year. The two sides—quizzically named the bananas and the oranges—refused to budge at all.

The new constitution got shot down by a margin of 57% to 43%, which wasn't a big deal really, but what was a big deal was the peace that followed. People got awfully ticked in 2000 when Bush eeked past Gore, but riots and pandemonium didn't spread across the States. Why is peace such a big deal here then? Or, a better question, why is violence so normal?

The ruling party in Kenya is not founded on political ideals or religious beliefs; the ruling party is Kikuyu, the largest tribe in Kenya (over 20% of the population). Every president in Kenya's independent history has been Kikuyu. Do you want to guess what the second biggest party is? Yup, the second largest tribe. In this election, 97% of Kikuyus voted in favor of the new constitution. All of the other tribes combined far outnumber the Kikuyus though. About 90% of non-Kikuyu voted against the constitution. You can see how the final tally came to be what it was.

It got me to thinking about my own affiliations. As an American, my loyalty is to my conscience, my beliefs, and, in a sense, to myself. I'm an ethnic mix of European ancestry personally, and my country is dubbed the melting pot because of its own lack of homogenous culture. Except for my loyalty to Christ's kingdom, my political affiliation could change at any time with little repercussion. Here though, tribal lines run the deepest of any affiliation. Even Christianity has had trouble permeating these loyalties. The century-old Christian church here is just starting to send missionaries to other tribes—a monumental feat in the eyes of locals.

I can't imagine living in a truly war-torn land, where your very survival was a question mark. Some of my students understand this reality, and I pray they'll all make it back safely from being with their families over the Christmas season.

Peace on Earth: it doesn't mean anything to you until your corner of the world is threatened. I'm thankful for peace tonight.

*december 7—kenya's cats

Heather brought more than groceries home from Nairobi yesterday; she brought home a Christmas present for our whole family. While Africa is well known for its big cats (leopards, lions, and cheetahs), we now have a little kitten—Kiama.

Kiama means "miracle" in Kikuyu, and we chose the name together with Susan. Susan thought it an appropriate name because of the situation the cat came from. People in Nairobi stand out along the streets with a litter full of kittens and try to sell them to the people waiting in traffic. You can probably imagine what some poor people might buy the animals for, and if they don't sell, the sellers simply kill them. Susan thought it was a miracle that this cat ended up with us, in a good home, with trips to the vet, and not in a skillet. We, on the other hand, think "miracle" is a good name because if this tiny kitten survives Micah (our 20 month old) it *will* be a miracle.

Heather's got a soft spot in her heart for cats, having had one cat or another throughout most of her life. Our cat in the States, a tan Persian named Moses, was supposed to catch up with us here when Heather's parents visit in December of '06. Unfortunately, international airlines have changed their policies, and no longer allow small pets to travel as carry-ons. They can travel, but they must go as cargo, and the fee is well over a thousand dollars. We were unwilling to pay that price for a cat (even if it was Heather's baby and a wedding gift from her uncle), so we decided to get a new one. K-K (our nickname for Kiama, pronounced kay-kay) cost $7 off the street, and after veterinarian visits, she'll still cost us less than $50. Affordable and, of course, terribly cute.

K-K is doing great. She's getting used to being carried around by her head (by Micah), and she's already been baptized (last night Micah took her into the bathroom and dropped her in the toilet). Don't worry though; she's fighting back with claws and teeth, prompting Micah to say, "No bite!" Everything is play to a kitten, and Micah is just her big brother—pounding her and torturing like any loving brother would do.

Yes, our cat has been aptly named. Miracle.

*december 13—where the wild things are

Kiama isn't the only wild creature in our life.

We also have lizards, spiders, flying beetles, mosquitoes, moths, and termites. This is to be expected in Africa, right? Yeah, I'd think so too, but you see, these are the critters that we have in our house—not out in the wild. Let me introduce our neighbors.

Our front door is big, sturdy, and wooden, but it's also about 2 inches too short for the doorway. Hence, visiting lizards stop by to say hi on occasion.

We live in a concrete block house, but there are many cracks and holes in the walls where urchins of various size and species live. I wouldn't be surprised to see spiders generally; they live everywhere. What's a bit frightening is that every spider I see is of a different kind. Ones with red eyes, skinny big ones, thick little ones, speedy ones—all kinds. You'd think after having been here six months we'd have seen 'em all. Nope. There goes a new one up my curtain as I type.

Without screens on our windows, flying guests love to drop in, especially at night when they see our lights on. The flying beetles are the size of a walnut, buzz like a mini-chainsaw, and couldn't navigate themselves out of a paper bag, let alone our house. The infamous mosquitoes are rare at our elevation, but they accurately heard that our bathroom is a warm, wet place. Moths are a frequent accessory to the sole of my nearest shoe.

Our house is converted from an old dorm, so there are many makeshift wooden walls. You know what that means. We're serenaded each night by the rhythmic munching of termites in our ceiling, which is only slightly less annoying than a Chinese soldier dripping water on your forehead. At this point they've only bored through four holes, but I'm guessing they'll get to double digits before the maintenance guys do anything about it.

We haven't seen any big mice or rats yet (although our kitten did manage to kill a small mouse on Tuesday), but we're ready. I've been practicing my technique. I spy the unwanted intruder, I jump up on a chair, and I scream like a little girl. Works every time.

*december 16—the commercial spirit

"How are we supposed to get in the Christmas spirit without advertisements to help us?"

This question (asked by my lovely wife) had us both in stitches at dinner the other night. It was a joke, but it was very sincere. I laughed at its shallowness, but I truly feel the same as she. There are no billboards, no sidewalk decorations, no store displays, no barrage of commercials to help us artificially get in the "spirit" of Christmas. So what are we to do, we ex-pats away from home at Christmas time?

We have a tree up, which helps. We've got a handful of Christmas CDs to listen to. We've been sent some Christmas presents from church friends and family members. That's what we have going for us.

Here's what's not going for us. It's getting warmer here. Days are in the 80's, mostly sunny and dry. Our families and friends are, oh, about ten thousand miles away, and we'll be spending the holidays with brand new people. We are miles and miles away from the commercial center (Nairobi) and won't be doing a lot of Christmas shopping in our free time. We don't have a TV. (*Does Target have cool holiday commercials again this year?* How would we know?) No *Charlie Brown Christmas*, no *It's a Wonderful Life*. No commercialism. We're sunk.

Of course, I write this all very tongue-in-cheek. Christmas isn't about gifts and commercialism and decorations. Right? The Christmas spirit is about something deep and special. *Right?*

I'm not sure if we'll find our holiday cheer this year. It's going to be harder to remember the reason for the season without all of our cultural prompts around us. But I'm wondering now if what I labeled the "Christmas spirit" was really about Christ at all. Or was it more of a 50/50, spiritual/cultural split?

It's going to be interesting to experience Christmas for the first time in Kenya. Maybe it will be richer and truer, or maybe it will be lame. I don't know. But I'm hoping the season is better without all of those advertisements distorting the real spirit of Christmas.

*december 20—Christmas presents

Christian came home from the hospital yesterday, after nearly a month's stay. Heather talked to her brother over the weekend, and he said that the little man turned a corner at the end of last week. His stools were normal and he was eating 50 ml. of formula and more! He was smiling and had much more energy. We're so joyful and thankful to God for this healing and this mercy on us all.

To add to all this joy, we also found out that three of our best friends/couples are expecting. The Doughtertys in San Diego, the Harrises in Georgia, and the Hulls in Lesotho, South Africa.

What better Christmas gifts could there be? A healed and healthy family and the news of more precious ones on the way!

*december 24—because Christ has come

We have a few holiday events planned with friends here as we all try not to miss friends, family, and traditions of home too much. Caroling at the children's ward of the Kijabe Hospital and then a candle light service on Christmas Eve help get us in the mood, but nothing can substitute for family. We'd be foolish though if we focused on the pain and longing, even if this will be our most depressing Christmas ever, bar none. But rather than focus on that, we're trying to focus on our purpose for being here half a world away—to see Jesus Christ lifted up in all the Earth and in the lives of the 500 students at Rift Valley Academy.

*december 25—shadows and sunshine

I've been dying to get the new Switchfoot CD. They are a San Diego band that I've seen a dozen times in concert. I heard it was coming out back in October, and I even asked a few people to send it to me as an early Christmas present. No luck. But now, Christmas is actually here, and it has come in the mail thanks to my sister. I'm so stoked.

One song of theirs has been rattling around in my head this week. It's called "The shadow proves the sunshine." The shadows in my life right now are everywhere. They're not overwhelming but are very persistent. Most of them deal with

Heather's family. They've had a tough run. First, Heather left them to come here. House problems linger for her parents ever since the San Diego wildfires of 2003. Heather's Grandpa died. Christian was near death.

We're feeling worried and sad and a bit guilty because we're not there. It's weird having a life that's so scattered. San Diego, Pennsylvania, Kijabe. It's hard to be 100% anywhere. Another shadow.

And then there's the loneliness. We're here so we need new relationships even as we keep in touch with old friends. But friendships take time and seasons. Time we have little of in this hectic world and seasons take years to come by. Loneliness is a shadow.

I have hope that the first year here will be true to first years' natures. Hard. And then things will improve. If so, I'm one-third through it. The shadow of the first year blues. Then add in the fact that I'm in another country, and that pretty much completes the picture.

But there can't be shadows without light. And I know the light is there. So bright and beautiful. Christ shines down on us even here. Giving love and hope. The shadows prove the sunshine.

*december 29—you're so fat!

It's that time of year again. Time for resolutions and diets and the return of self-control in our food consumption. You may have thought the words "You're so fat" about yourself, but hopefully you haven't heard anyone say it. Those would not be nice words to hear, would they? Well, maybe not to you, but they are to a Kenyan.

Susan and Heather were baking in the kitchen around Christmas when Susan got to talking about something her friends have been telling her. They say, "Susan, you are getting so fat. Heather must be feeding you well."

This was a high compliment for Susan; she asked Heather if Heather thought she was getting fat too. Heather couldn't get the words out; she'd been so conditioned to be polite and to *never* comment on a woman's increase in weight. Susan was sad. She was fishing for a compliment, but Heather wouldn't (couldn't!) give it.

Susan said she understood. There was once a white woman who was attending her church. After a lengthy illness where she was near death, the woman began to recover. She came back to church, and everyone was very happy to see her. They all told her how fat she looked. The woman lowered her head and began to cry what they thought were tears of joy over her recovery. They weren't tears of joy, as you can imagine.

That was the first time Susan learned that other cultures see their weight and body image differently than hers, and she understands that Heather might not be too happy if she ever tells her, "You're looking awfully plump today!" Heather and she actually came to an agreement: if Susan will constantly tell Heather how svelt she looks, Heather will tell Susan how rotund she's getting. Everybody wins.

It's fascinating how cultures can be so different. In one culture everyone can afford to eat and eat a lot so the challenge is *not* to get fat amidst all the excess. Most Americans need time to exercise and to buy and prepare the healthiest foods (not the cheap junk or fast foods) and need money to purchase sports equipment (or a gym membership) to keep trim.

In another culture few can afford to eat abundantly, and there is no extra money for the fattening (but tasty) foods. If you do get enough to eat, you probably have to work so hard that you burn every last calorie. To have time to relax and to have enough food to eat is the way to get fat, and fat is good.

A cliché fits well here: beauty lies in the eye of the beholder. Well, Kenyan beholders like their beautiful figures full and fat. And that, my friends, is the ticket to being guilt-free after the holiday binging—move to Kenya.

*january 4—american football is a kenyan nightmare

One of the things that missionaries are supposed to do when they cross cultures is learn the hobbies and pastimes of the natives. I'm supposed to be learning how to play cricket and rugby and falling in love with the other football (what we call soccer in the U.S.). However, you won't find me tearing my shirt off, running around, and yelling, "GOOOOAAAAALLLLL!" any time soon. No, I'm an unabashed bad missionary who is still in love with college football. And this time of the year is football season in America.

My love started early. The first tears of joy I ever shed? January 1, 1987, when Penn State upset Miami for the national championship. Although my team has had a rough go of it so far in the new millennium, this year they soared again. It's been hard being a fan from half a world away, but I have persevered, thanks to the Internet and a fellow Lions fan.

The Internet made it possible to listen to the games that were being broadcast on American radio stations. Granted, the games didn't start until at least 8 p.m. at night and sometimes kept me up till the wee hours of morning, but those were minor inconveniences for a true fan. Then, a few weeks after the games were played, my childhood friend Andy would send me a DVD of the game from Pennsylvania. By that time I'd forgotten most of the game so it was like watching it anew. What bliss!

If you have any nose for sports, you've probably heard about how well Penn State did this year. After all those losing seasons and the petitions to fire old Coach Paterno, they surprised the nation and won all but one game this season. Their bowl game vs. Florida State last night stole the national sports spotlight, and all eyes were on the Orange Bowl in Miami. Even my African eyes.

Our campus has a satellite dish and a subscription with a South African cable company. The student lounge has a TV, and if you talk to the dean of students, he will turn the channel on that TV. Not surprisingly, there is little demand for the TV at 4 a.m., which is exactly when the PSU-FSU game began here in Kenya; thus, I was able to watch my beloved team play *live* from the middle of Africa. Seem too good to be true? Read on.

The game came on just as promised, and in my sleepy stupor, I marveled at the shiny box that carried me to a faraway world called Florida. The game went slowly, with all of the TV hype and halftime show drudgery, and there was still a lot of game to be played when, unexpectedly and tragically, the satellite went off. The screen read "E16 is currently scrambled." I waited and waited, sure that this was just a normal, temporary African outage. It wasn't. The game, my precious game, was gone.

Since the kids are back on campus and school is in session, I walked home at dawn this morning and got ready, with no time to check the Internet to see the final score. I taught my first few classes, still anxiously unaware, when a fellow American football pilgrim found me. He brought tidings of great joy—the game would be replayed on TV at 2 p.m. that afternoon. There was still hope. I might see the game yet, if only the satellite would be restored.

The dean of students later found me and told me what had happened. The school had forgotten to pay its cable bill, and rather than warn RVA about being overdue, the company shut it off. At 7 a.m. on January 4 (during the end of the PSU game) of all the possible times! Some days it's not good to be a Murphy and to have that darn law named after you.

This story though does have a happy ending. I watched the game (still not knowing the outcome) that afternoon after school, and Penn State won in triple overtime against the Criminals…I mean…the Seminoles of Florida State. I didn't cry any tears this time; I couldn't. This whole saga of following my childhood team from a distant country despite all kinds of crazy obstacles (i.e. sporadic Internet radio, month old DVDs,

cancelled cable subscriptions) is too funny to cry. Ahh, the
things we do for love…

*january 5—cultural blinders

Ethnocentricity is succinctly defined as the belief that
your culture is the correct one. Let me just raise my hand right
now. I'm guilty of ethnocentricity.

I was reading from the Old Testament today about the
time when David was trying to escape King Saul's plot to kill
him. He tells Jonathan to pass along this excuse for his
absence—I've gone to Bethlehem for a clan sacrifice. My
thought was *What kind of lame excuse is that? Clan sacrifice,
where did you get that one? Why not tell the king you had to go
wash your hair? That'd be more believable.*

But then I thought back to something we just
experienced here. We recently attended a "clan" gathering of
Susan's family. Her cousins and uncles came from as far away
as Nairobi (quite a journey without your own vehicle) to be
together for a special holiday. It wasn't even a big holiday, just
one of the dozen or so in Kenya, but still they gathered from far
and wide to be together. I helped slaughter my first goat, and
Heather rolled out chapatis (thick tortillas) and cut vegetables.
We ate and ate, the ladies and children danced, and everyone
played games. Unfortunately we had to leave before dark, but
the party was still going strong into the evening.

Family is important. Families gather. Everyone
understands that here. David had a great excuse. Saul bought it
(for the most part), and I should've, too. A clan gathering, a
family event, was and is no small matter.

I've got a long way to go, but thank God my American
blinders are falling off a bit more each day.

*january 8—another term begins

It's hard to believe that it's January 8th already and that
it's 2006 already. Three years ago this time we were working
hard at teaching, kidless, and fixing up our home in San Diego;

two years ago we were still praying about where God would have us go and were expecting a baby; and last year we were moving out of our home and preparing for Africa. It's good for the heart to reflect on what God's has done for us.

With the weeks off in December we got so much work done while getting rejuvenated, too. We actually feel *prepared* for this term, and for teachers, being more than a few days ahead with our classes is such a relief. We have most of the same students (a couple have left because of family furloughs and a bunch came, returning from their furloughs), but due to the long break, it really feels like we're starting from scratch.

This term has some new opportunities for us. I am going to be teaching a sophomore Sunday School class on masculinity with three other staff members and working with the student outreach committee to plan and organize events for the student body. Heather's going to be helping with recreational activities on the weekends and cooking dinners for students one night a week in our home.

We will also be continuing our responsibilities from last term—teaching English and guitar for Ryan and History for Heather, Kikuyu lessons, relieving dorm parents one night a week, helping with various worship teams, speaking at student chapels, and hosting a small group in our home three times per term.

Last week, we had Community Day, which RVA hosts in conjunction with the local church. Games, food, and speakers. It's a fun event for the residents of Kijabe, and it drew about 300 people this year. My favorite game was the tug-of-war. On my side, 50 strong and healthy Kenyan men. On the other end of the rope, about 100 women. Yes, they did beat the men in the second and third pull. But I must add that they took about half of our guys away after we dominated the first pull. It's my humble opinion that it's rigged every year so that the ladies win. I'll be lifting weights this year to avenge our loss though, and I'll let you know what happens next year.

*january 12—a prayer

Fascinating. At the same time as I am starting to feel comfortable here with the rhythms and routines of teaching and living, I'm beginning to deeply miss family, friends, and home culture. I guess we're transitioning into the permanent phase of our move or maybe just I am. It's no longer a trip or a temporary adventure. A visit with our friends is not just around the corner. A retreat from here to our home town is nowhere near the horizon. Holidays with loved ones aren't a few months away. We're here. "They" and "it" are over there, and "this" is the permanent state of life now.

God, be near us as we cope with this change. Be strong for Heather as this is her first transition. Give us a love for RVA and a contentment. Temper our homesickness. Amen.

*january 14—ryan's pants

It'll be interesting to see how long the clothing supply that we brought with us to Africa lasts. We didn't go crazy in our pre-field shopping, but we felt well prepared. One of the things I brought was an old pair of tan corduroys, but these are more than just pants—they are a tangible life lesson for me.

These pants were offered to me about five years ago by a friend named Ryan Stasko, and I've never been one to turn down anything preceded with the adjective "free." About a year later, he came to San Diego for our wedding and we got burnt at the beach together a few days before the big event—a special memory for me. A few months later, Ryan developed a brain tumor and went through chemo and surgeries over the course of a few years—to no avail. He passed away a year ago this week, but his life, his memory, and his example live on.

Ryan looked at his suffering as a strange blessing from God. He said, "God must think I'm a pretty strong person to give me this to deal with." His attitude in the face of his illness was nothing short of angelic, and the peace he had in God made me envious. Ryan went to be with Christ at 23.

You might think it's morbid to be talking about Ryan's pants, but for me it's inspirational. When I wear them I think of him and the impact his life had on so many, and I think of how short life is. On mornings when I'm struggling or discouraged, I see those pants on the hanger and remember that God must think I'm a pretty special person to give me this _____ (fill in the blank with whatever I'm struggling with that day) to deal with. It's my responsibility to do as much with my life as I can because Ryan can't, to love others deeply and sincerely each day of my numbered days. And when those days are done, Ryan will find me in heaven and share more with me.

This is a song that I wrote a few days before he died last year. It's called "Past the sun and the moon."

I heard you're not doing well
You've been down for a spell
These short days have felt so long
The whole universe seems wrong

These flowers and those cards
Remind you of a life less hard
Kind kisses and fine quips
Off of everyone's lips

Isn't it strange how goodbye
Brings the tears to our eyes
For a homecoming sweet
All the love you will meet

No matter what happens next
You know all the rest

You'll feel better soon
Past the sun and the moon
You'll feel better soon
Past the sun and the moon

*january 17—a hospital for the world

Earlier, I mentioned the local hospital, and when I say "local" I mean "local." I can see the hospital gate from my bedroom window. It's probably 200 yards down the hill. The hospital is run by the Africa Inland Church (the denomination that has resulted from the work of AIM) and is considered one of the top hospitals in East Africa. I know someone who lived in Uganda (a 2 hour flight or 12 hour drive away) and came to Kijabe Hospital to deliver a baby. That's how good this hospital is.

It's run by an amalgam of Kenyan professionals, long term missionaries, and short term volunteers. There are dozens of beds, operating rooms (called Theaters), and an emergency room area (ominously called Casualty). Just west of the main hospital is an annex called Bethany Children's Hospital (originally Crippled's was used instead of Children's, sadly), and north of the hospital is a dentist's office where the main dentist is a grad of UNC and Duke (if you follow college basketball, you know that clearly he's a confused man).

Walking through the hospital you'll find an array of outfits rarely found outside of Halloween in the States. You have Muslim women with only eyes showing, Masai people with plaid wraps covering their nudity, Indians in suits, and nurses dressed in traditional blue dresses. This diversity is precisely where the ministry of the hospital comes in to play. Obviously, the staff is ministering to sick and hurting bodies and bringing healing in the name of the true Physician. As a hospital though in the middle of a needy place, all kinds of folks are drawn here, including unreached people groups.

A few weeks ago a Somali man (largely a Muslim people group) was at the hospital for surgery and in talking to the staff and chaplains, he accepted Christ. Conversion is a remarkable event, but when you realize what this could mean for his fellow Muslims and to his standing in the Muslim community, it is even more amazing. As he tells others about how God gave him new life through his Son, who knows what impact this man will have on his family/community/etc.? He could bring others to eternal life through faith, or it could bring about the end of his family and his acceptance in his village and even martyrdom. Or all of the above could happen. Conversion for Muslims is no small matter. But whatever the future holds, the Spirit is at work.

They come to the hospital; they go out healed and transformed. Sounds like an encounter with Jesus, doesn't it?

This isn't to say that we don't need to reach out to the unreached, but I found it interesting that God will on occasion bring the unreached to us. As the Muslim extremists tear up Third World countries with terrorism and genocide, we're seeing more and more exiles moving away from homelands, possibly coming to your backyard. If the lost and unreached come to you, will you be ready, like Kijabe Hospital, to care for their material needs and offer them the knowledge of God that they are dying for?

*january 24—networking

The network of people involved with missions is elaborate. As a teacher, I fall into the category of "support" missionaries. I'm only here because "frontline" missionaries are translating the Bible and planting churches and caring for the sick. There are others like me—pilots, buyers, administrators, logistics people, etc.. I knew all about these people before, but not until I got here did I find out about another layer of "support" that's in place.

Susan is a support person to us. Her work and service free up so much time and energy for us to serve the MKs here at RVA. She spends about 10 hours a week doing chores around the house and some basic cooking, and she watches Micah about 14 hours a week while we are teaching. That is 24 extra hours that we get to give for the kids and their parents who are on the frontlines.

In some ways, life is not as simple here. Everything takes longer, and rarely does anything go smoothly. You make many food items from scratch, and the closest grocery store is in Nairobi. Electricity is expensive, so it's cheaper to line dry your clothes than to buy a drier and pay through the nose (although they are available in the city). Of course, there are no dishwashers, and if there were, they would be a waste of water and electricity. This more time-consuming life would mean less time for us to do what we've been called to do if we didn't have help.

Without Susan, some area of our lives would have to fold. We could not find the time to do all that we do. I couldn't help with student outreach projects, or Heather would have to give up helping the high school worship band. We wouldn't be able to supervise our friends' dormitory one night a week to give them a break. I wouldn't be able to sit down and play with my son at night. We wouldn't be able to teach 11 classes between the two of us. Heather wouldn't be involved with the women's Bible study. We'd never be able to lead worship for church or student chapels. The list goes on. Something would have to give.

Susan is an essential support for what we do here.

Sure, Susan and the other national workers here at RVA could view their jobs as just that—jobs. In the past, this has been a tendency. They get a steady, quality job from good employers, and that's it. It's a job. We're trying to instill in our workers that they are more than just employees; they are a crucial part of missions in their country and beyond their country. In the same way that I support frontline missionaries, they support me. If one rung of the ladder falters, new heights will never be reached.

*january 26—transportation problems

The weekend is approaching, food is getting low, and diapers are becoming scarce…so Heather starts the hunt to find a ride into town, begging, pleading, praying for a ride from someone with a car. Most long term missionaries here at RVA own cars (35 out of 40 couples) and make trips into town every other week for supplies. For those of us who don't own a car yet, rental cars are available for us to use (3 cars for 26 people). However, on most weekends those rental cars are all booked.

This week however, an unusual blessing—during Staff Chai (equivalent to an American coffee break) someone offers three empty seats to go into town. Heather's hand shoots up so fast that she's the second one to claim a seat. Thank goodness, she's going to town for supplies!

It's Saturday afternoon and off they go. While in town, the driver does not need to go to the main grocery store, and she is on a tight schedule for stops. Therefore Heather makes her purchases (three weeks worth!) at smaller shops in the area, and only has 40 minutes accomplish the task! If that's not challenging enough, she has Micah with her because I have school activities that day. This trip was a success though. The ladies and she had great fellowship, safety on the roads, and a chance to get needed supplies for the weeks ahead.

Our next trip in two weeks is already planned out, as we have reserved a car. A car rental costs over $50 per trip so we try to share the expense with another couple or two singles. It's rare to see a car go to town half empty.

Experienced missionaries suggested not getting a car right away. We're so glad we haven't. It's given us time to focus on language learning, curriculum development, and adjusting to our new culture. However, a vehicle is a real need for our lives here so we are going to let our supporters know about this need and, if enough funds come in, we hope to buy one next summer.

Reasons for needing a car abound, besides the ones in the story above. Students have extra-curricular activities (from sports to choir trips to ministry outreach) where they need rides off campus. Every beginning of term, midterm, and end of term kids need rides to their planes or buses or directly to their parents' homes. Besides the personal needs like food and supplies, most of our banking and government business happen in Nairobi, which is an hour's drive. Without a car, we are not able to help and actually place extra burdens on other folks here.

Cars here are more expensive. A car that would barely go for $1,000 in the States cost $4,000 for one missionary here. Cars hold their resale value very well too because of the scarcity of them. The problem with buying used is that, unless you have records of all previous owners and *trust* those owners, you don't know if the odometer has been tampered with.

Buying an inexpensive car is a good temporary solution but also a dangerous one. Back in August, we were broken down for two hours, and it wasn't until twilight that someone drove the hour from RVA to come pick us up. No one should be away from home at night in Africa, especially not along side of the road, and we were dangerously close to that predicament. I've heard countless other stories of people being stranded, some in literal life or death situations, because of a broken down car. Carjacking and armed burglaries are common as well. The roads are dangerous, the drivers are dangerous, and the towns we're going through are dangerous—all the more reason to have a vehicle that won't break down frequently in the first few months that you own it.

Let me tell you what some recent experiences have been for those who have bought vehicles for under $20,000. In the last 9 months, three new missionaries on limited budgets like ours have bought cars for under 20k—two Toyota Landcruisers and one Toyota mini-van. All three have spent weeks at the mechanics and have put a thousand more dollars into their vehicles. So there are two options: buy cheap and pay in time and money with repairs, while possibly putting your family in a perilous situation. Or pay the money to get a reliable vehicle.

Some of the priorities we have for our purchase: a newer car with low mileage and few owners, four wheel drive (especially necessary in the rainy season), high clearance (you think you've seen potholes?), seating for 7 (room for our family to grow and for student/staff passengers), good mileage, and a manufacturer with readily available parts (nobody has "driven a Ford lately" in Kenya). Our target price range is $25k-$30k. I know, I know. That sounds like it's gotta be bling-bling, but it's not. That's just a basic, used 4WD vehicle in good condition in Kenya.

Unfortunately, a car loan isn't a possibility. Remember, we are already living off monthly donations, and in order to pay for such a loan, we'd have to ask for at least $400 more in monthly support. Raising all of the money at once and forking over the rest from our own pockets is the only real solution.

We have $8,000 from selling our two cars in the States, and we already have $4,000 earmarked towards a car, gifts from different donors. There is a long way to go for this to be possible, and it's really lame to have to ask for everything. Humbling actually. But such is the missionary life, and we're convinced that somehow, some way God will find a way.

*january 31—what a hamburger is all about

In-n-out Burger is the place for the best burgers if you're ever on the West Coast of the U.S. I miss those burgers and those fries and those shakes. Man, do I miss them! Just singing their theme song makes my mouth water. *"In-n-out, that's what a hamburger's all about!"*

But that's not what I'm thinking of today when I think of in and out. I'm thinking about the hospital. I'll start with the *out*.

We found out three days ago that our nephew Christian was back in the hospital with more stomach problems and dehydration. But today's email brought good news. He is out of the hospital. He was discharged on Monday, and although he's very underweight and on a special diet, at least he's not in the hospital anymore. His whole family (grandparents included) is still recovering from the flu and that doesn't help his recovery either.

Now, the *in*.

Susan was sick last night, but she decided to come to work today anyway. On the way here, she collapsed with pains in her side and trouble breathing. They took her to the hospital down the hill. After tests and x-rays, the docs diagnosed her with pneumonia. We went to see her this afternoon (the hospital rooms here have 8 beds in them), and she was in a lot of pain. She was glad to see her little Micah though. To top it off, her daughter is scheduled to have her tonsils removed tomorrow! Her friend, Lois, will be watching Micah for us while Susan is ill, so that is a great blessing. Without her partnership, our work here would really be sunk.

What a week for her family! And I'm starting to include myself in that group. She's more than just a worker. Our lives are now tied together in that she is the beloved "tata" for Micah and in that we are helping her family to survive and thrive financially. Family.

I understand that it's hard to grasp the concept of house workers if you're not immersed in it. You'll have to trust me when I say that if this relationship is done right, with love, respect, and a sense of purpose flowing from both the employee and employer, then having a house worker is an enormous blessing for all involved.

FIVE

the rains down in africa

FEBRUARY-MARCH 2006

We're at the end of the dry season. There aren't seasons like North America here—cool fall, cold winter, pretty spring, hot summer. It's pretty much dry or wet. This year our dry season started early and has been more dry than normal, which means hard times for the rural people of Kenya.

Without water, wells dry up. When wells dry up, people have to travel farther to get water. When those wells get increased business, they dry up faster. Eventually, there is no water for miles and miles.

Without water, grass and shrubs and weeds die. Without wild greenery, there is no food for the livestock. Without food for the livestock (even if they survive the lack of water), they become more susceptible to disease and malnourishment.

Without healthy animals, there is no milk, eggs, or meat for the people. Without animal food sources, people must rely on crops. But of course, there are no thriving crops, so there is little food whatsoever for the people. Without food, people become more susceptible to disease and malnourishment.

The exact placement of RVA is a gift of providence. We live on the escarpment, or the side of the mountain. The good side of the mountain…the rainy side of the mountain. During the rainy season, this place resembles Seattle or a rain forest without the heat. It's acquired the nickname "school in the clouds" because there is a hovering fog for the rainy half of the year. We have numerous wells here on campus, and we're able to bathe and do laundry and wash dishes and even keep gardens. Usually.

Even though we live in one of the lush places in Kenya, we're currently on strict water conservation. The drought is so bad that our pumps have been running 24 hrs. straight for the past 5 weeks, and our wells are getting near crisis level. We're on laundry restrictions (underwear only), shower restrictions (1 minute each), and garden restrictions (only trapped laundry, kitchen, and bathroom water for plants and vegetables). And the bawdy rhyme "if it's yellow let it mellow; if it's brown flush it down" is our school motto as well.

To our Western tastes, these are inconveniences, but I see it as a small sacrifice considering what our neighbors in the valley below must deal with. In fact, I think we should be on water restrictions year round. Why should we be wasteful during the rainy season when we have no idea how dry the dry season will be? The more water we don't take from the earth, the more there will be for others in the valley below. Just because we have the water in our well and in the water table beneath us, it doesn't mean we should take as much.

You may be asking why Africa doesn't *do something* about their constant famines and droughts. To answer that question, we'd need to look deeper into the African worldview.

*february 4—the wrong answer

Not a few distant observers have asked why African countries constantly suffer from drought, famine, and disease. Is it only because of the desolate land on which they live? Is it the fault of corrupt leaders who horde and steal from their own needy people? Who is to blame for times like these?

Of course, as the insightful 20th century journalist H.L. Mencken said, "For every complex problem there is an answer that is clear, simple, and wrong." I, of all people, do not claim to have any answer here, but I do know one place the finger should point.

Many of the problems Africans have today have been passed down by their ancestors. These are not physical problems though, like debt or arid climates or primitive farming techniques. No, it's the attitude or worldview that most Africans embrace which has been passed down to them through the generations. Now, I could go into a lengthy history lesson of why these beliefs have emerged (which would make my history loving wife very pleased), but I'll only take the time to hit on the key points.

The history of Africa is a history of survival. When you're not sure where your next meal is coming from or whether your children will survive the most recent outbreak, you spend little time worrying about major issues which may or may not come in the future. You micromanage everything; nothing is macromanaged. Or to put it another way, worry about today and let tomorrow figure itself out. (Sounds like something Jesus said, doesn't it?) But with everyone worrying about their own small problems (or at largest, their tribe's problems), no one is looking out for the good of everyone. The leaders too (sometimes even elected ones) only look out for the interest of a minority of the people (usually their tribe).

The belief: take care of yourself today because tomorrow may never come. So this is the African worldview. What's the application? Well, let me start off by offering a comparison.

I lived in San Diego the past 10 years. San Diego is a desert. San Diego, however, never lacks for water. There is rationing at times, but nothing extreme. Why? Well, some politicians decided years ago that if the West Coast were to flourish, they'd need water. Somehow they finagled massive amounts from the Colorado River through pipes into LA and San Diego. Massive infrastructure was planned, paid for, and built. Mexico got shafted in the process as the once fertile delta by the Gulf of California is now desert, but America planned ahead and therefore thrived.

I give this example to juxtapose the Western way with the African way. The Western way is to prepare for long term survival. Today is taken care of: there's food in the kettle, able leaders on the throne, and a stable way of life. We've been afforded the ability to look ahead, to plan, and to prepare, and this has become a part of our psyche. We build aquaducts for fear of drought; the typical African enjoys the seasons of rain and leaves to tomorrow the fears and worries. When an entire nation or civilization espouses this relaxed attitude though, that is when problems ensue.

There is a drought today. Hundreds are dying, and hundreds more will die, but if this nation was to experience a week of torrential rains that filled up the streams and the wells, it would be as if there was never a drought at all. There would be rejoicing, and the drought would be forgotten, which isn't bad in itself. Unfortunately, the future threat of drought is also quickly forgotten, and the suffering would happen soon again.

How should we respond as Westerners when our fellow man is in need? What is our role in this whole cycle of poverty and poor planning and relief? Is there any hope?

*february 7—effective strategies

You probably have heard the Chinese proverb, "Give a man a fish and you feed him for a day. Teach a man to fish and you feed him for a lifetime." This serves as a great analogy for understanding how the West has tried to help Africa.

Aid organizations (as well as missions) have developed two main arms—relief and development. Relief is when you intervene with necessary food or medical supplies in extreme circumstances, and development is when you grow programs and teach techniques to avoid the extreme circumstances from ever taking place. Sometimes the two get lumped together, but it's very hard for any organization to do both. It's human nature to rather enjoy taking a fish and to dislike learning how to fish for yourself.

Our mission agency tries to steer clear of relief. Relief can be a money pit. Many mission agencies have fallen into the trap of becoming sources of relief, which keeps them from doing the spiritual work that they originally set out to do and actually hurts those in need. If it's perceived that the fish supply is endless, why learn how to fish?

Money is no solution for the problems the typical African faces. Strategy, foresight, and development come closer to the answer. Relief is a band-aid; development is surgery.

(This doesn't mean that my co-workers and I don't pour time and money into relieving immediate needs around us; it just means that the purpose of our work is not to give away food, water, clothing, medicine, etc.)

One development strategy is well digging. Getting deep into the earth is impossible with human hands, but with the use of human invention, often costly human invention, the water below the surface is attainable. The cost of buying or renting such a machine is lucrative though, and without going into a whole explanation of government finances here, the problems are such: ownership, maintenance, distribution, and capital. These same problems can exist when development agencies and missions try to dig wells, but they can also be circumvented if done outside of the government context.

A mission agency can take care of the capital and ownerships issues by paying for it and making it the property of the local church. Maintenance and distribution then can be run through the local church, independent of outside help ideally, and if each cog in the machine does its job, a long term and effective solution can be found—a well-maintained, productive, lasting, and healthy source of water for the poor. There are other development strategies related to water as well (no pun intended), like farming techniques and seed replacement; each helps in its own right.

Eighty percent of all deaths in developing countries are water—or sanitary—related, and treating diseases caused by unsafe water and poor sanitation cost the equivalent of $20 billion every year (*Relevant*, Nov/Dec 2005). Clean water is a huge problem and is worth developing programs to help. Why wait to cure the preventable diseases after they occur? Why not take care of the root problem? Why send food to drought-ridden countries when it's too late? Why spend thousands of dollars on relief when that same money can be spent on development which will make the relief unnecessary?

We cannot cure every glitch in the African worldview or every symptom of poverty which plagues them, but we can use our resources and our insights to develop programs that will save lives, will promote health, and will function successfully in the African context.

*february 8—adam's apples

While eating in the caf, I spotted one of my squirmy students with an entire tray filled with apples. My gut reaction was to yell at him; students are not supposed to take food with them out of the cafo. A stockpile of apples like that could only be destined for one thing—a clandestine burglary. I got up from my table and began to head towards Adam, who was eating all by himself and was quite oblivious of my approach, when I had a different idea. Rather than scold this kid, I should invite him to sit with us. Not mentioning the bushel of apples on his tray, I invited him to sit with Heather, Micah, and me. Adam accepted and carefully walked his loaded tray to our table.

We had a nice lunch, found out about his siblings and his parents' ministry, and really got to see a different side of Adam. He's smart and polite and always thinking. Socially though, he's very backward, both in his classroom behavior with teachers and in outside of class with his classmates and dorm brothers. Getting yelled at, made fun of, and marginalized is kind of a way of life for him in the eighth grade. As we finished our lunches and got ready to go, Adam wasn't quite finished, but he was almost finished. Over the course of our lunch conversation, Adam had eaten an absurd amount of apples.

It was then that I realized that I got lucky. Where I had almost made a fool of myself and beaten down a kid who had been nothing but beaten down, I ended up having a great lunch and getting to know a kid better. He's one of my favorite students now, and I thank God for saving me from myself sometimes.

*february 9—money matters

So far, $3k has been given towards the vehicle fund. No other pledges have been made. We have one small church supporting us besides our home church in San Diego, but that's it. Overall, we don't have a huge financial base to draw from.

It's actually quite amazing that we're here on so little "church" support. Most of our monthly support comes from individuals, 67 individuals to be exact. The benefit of having many churches supporting you is that they usually give larger chunks of money out of their budgets. The downside is that you have to spread yourself very thin during visits home (2 weeks at this church, 2 weeks at that church, all over the place for months at a time), and it's harder to make connections with entire congregations of people.

The benefit of having more individual support is that it's much more personal. You are more connected and friendly with these people who are investing in your life and ministry. The downside is that individuals have smaller budgets and can only give a small portion of your total need.

This was a major dread of mine when considering becoming a missionary. I hate asking people for anything. I'm a terrible combination of shyness and pride. And money is the worst thing of all to have to ask for. I'm extreme in my Western-ness in this way. I want to be independent and self-sufficient and strong. Asking for money means weakness. Or at least, this is what I was thinking.

To compound this reticence, I thought that becoming a missionary meant that you needed to have 7, 8, 9 churches supporting you. That would mean 7, 8, or 9 places where I'd be a complete stranger and have shallow relationships every time we visited. I am socially awkward, especially with strangers, and I loathe shallow relationships, especially at church. I saw no way for a person like me to do what was necessary to become a missionary.

A book came across my path, however, called *Friend Raising*. It was written by this woman who was a missionary to Hawaii ("Rough life," you snicker), and her story was not about raising money but about nurturing friendships. Maybe she was like me and she hated being a stranger at a dozen churches. Or maybe she was just really good at loving people and having relationships. I don't know. But most of her financial support came from her friends and acquaintances that she made through the years. This book taught me important lessons about loving people back home even while I go "over there," and it showed me that even someone with my weaknesses could raise the funds to go. I have friends. Heather has friends. Great friends, and lots of them. We're lucky like that.

And that's how God provided the means for us to be here. Some give as little as $10 a month, one gives $300 a month. But it all adds up to keep us fed and sheltered and healthy here.

But this "extra" need of a car is spreading some of them thin. They are already giving so much, and I know they want to help, but it's hard. We'll wait and see what God has planned for us.

*february 10—the old self

There is a scene in *The Lord of the Rings* trilogy where Frodo uses the ring to become invisible and escape his enemies. But when he does, he finds that they are actually stronger and more deadly on the invisible, spiritual level. There, in his attempted escape, he is struck through the heart with a sword of one of the Wraiths. The wound cuts through both the physical and the spiritual level, and although it does not immediately kill him, it plagues him the rest of his days. He's opened himself up to a mortal wound that causes him severe pain and forces him to eventually leave the other Hobbits and go to die somewhere.

(At least, that's what I gathered from the movies. I never read the books, but please don't tell anyone. I am an English teacher after all.)

Well, I awoke last night from terrible dreams in which my past sins were being played out again in ultra-realistic fashion. And I thought of Frodo. Everything we do in this world has spiritual consequences, and so I too have wounds that I willingly received. Of course, I have asked for forgiveness and fully trust that God is faithful to do just that. 1 John 1 also says that God has cleansed me of all unrighteousness, but these dreams last night came seemingly from out of nowhere.

I guess I shouldn't be surprised by all of this. It's not like becoming a missionary could be a magical potion that makes all my problems disappear, although I'll admit it's been a naïve wish of mine. I'm sure you've done it too. If only I do _____ for God, then He'll take away _____. You fill in the blanks with your own proposal of the day. If only I donate to this charity, maybe God will give me a raise at work. If only I pray every night for my child, perhaps she'll start making better choices. If only, then. We've all done it with our petty little views of God.

Perhaps my little silent dream was "If only I sell everything and become a missionary, then He'll take away my struggle with sin." God doesn't play games like this, though. He's totally for our healing and for our growth, but there's no shortcut. It's a long painful process that involves daily dying on our part. Dying to the old self, believing that the new self is the true self. Choosing to obey today and letting the pain of yesterday fade away. This is the reality, not a dream.

*february 11—little love gifts

Since Valentine's Day is coming up and all, I thought I'd write a random tale of love for you. It might take a while to realize what this has to do with love, but persevere! You'll find it.

Appliances are becoming more and more available in Nairobi (Kenya's capitol city), and washing machines are now an affordable luxury (is that an oxymoron?) found in all of the missionaries' homes. While driers are also available, they are a little less practical. Besides the cost to buy one, the cost of electricity here is a weighty consideration. So, we have a washer but no drier. It's not that bad though. Four out of five days are suitable for line drying your clothes, and the wind here makes short work of wet clothes usually. If you've ever line dried your clothes though, you know what a shirt or a towel feels like after blowing in the wind for a few hours. Stiff. Cardboard-like. Painful. Heather really was peeved about the towels, which never really felt like towels until they were thoroughly saturated by your wet body. Not the cruelest torture imaginable but still a daily annoyance.

Then, something random happened. We had to move our medicines from the small cabinet in our bathroom to another room. The cabinet rested right on top of our water heater, and the high and humid temperatures weren't good for our medicines. So, we filled that space with our rigid towels instead and thought nothing else of it.

The next day, when one of us took a shower, we noticed an interesting thing—the towels were warm and soft when we reached for them. The water heater which was ruining our medicines was warming and softening our towels for us!

Is there anything better than turning off the shower and, before you can get cold, grabbing a soft, warm towel?

Some people would say I'm crazy for seeing God in something trivial like this, but I have to chuckle a "thank you" to Him when I get out of the shower in the morning. God makes me laugh sometimes. Little love gifts in the most unusual packages.

*february 14—sad morning

Jeff and Kate are new this year like us, and we've become good friends with them. Micah, Heather, and I got to meet their newborn son Colin on Saturday night. They sent out the e-mail below this morning.

Dear friends and family,

Job 1:21 "Naked I came from my mother's womb, and naked I will depart. The Lord gave and the Lord has taken away; may the name of the Lord be praised."

On February 10th at 8:44 p.m. our son Colin Makini was born. The name Makini means strength of character and gentleness. On the way to the hospital for his delivery, Jeff prayed that God would bless and use him, however long his life would be.

On February 13th in the evening, God took Colin home while he was sleeping. Being in Jeff's arms always calmed him, and now His Father in heaven is holding him.

Please pray for us. Pray that God would comfort us. Pray for God to be honored. Pray for our families as they receive the news. Pray that if it is possible, Kate's parents might be able to come out for the funeral. They do not have passports.

We ask that for now there be no visitors and no phone calls. Thank you for praying for us.

Jeff and Kate

*february 16—miracles in tragedy

This has been a hard week for everyone, as school continued on as normal despite this emotional bomb that exploded in our midst. Heather has been organizing all of the meals and snacks for Jeff and Kate's family, and she helped clean their house yesterday. They're planning the memorial service on Saturday and all of their immediate family is now in town. This was a *huge* miracle because Kate's parents didn't have passports. An exception was made and they arrived in Kenya today (Thursday)! They are in good spirits and praising God despite this painful loss. We haven't spent much time with them, but in our brief encounters (and everyone's) we're amazed at how God is carrying them through this. Tonight they are watching video footage of Colin's life with their family with our video projector.

*february 17—praise Him!

Kate spoke at our Friday chapel service to everyone's shock. She read the passage where Jesus enters Jerusalem to praises and the Jewish officials are upset. Jesus says, "If they don't praise me, the rocks will cry out!" She emphatically told over 600 people to praise God even in this, in a shaking, quivering voice. Once she was finished she crumbled at her seat with sobs, but she delivered a message of God's goodness to the community.

*february 18--celebration

The graveside service was at 2 p.m. on Saturday at the Kijabe cemetery for family only. Heather and I led a few songs for the service. The tombstone said "In 3 days he changed the world" and quoted Job. The Lord gave, the Lord has taken away. Blessed be the name of the Lord. Jeff went down into the grave to put his son's small cedar box in its final resting place. Not the job of any father, but one that he accepted as God's will.

The memorial service (they called it a celebration service) at the church was probably the most incredible service I've ever experienced. There were songs of grief and joy. There was a short message from the pastor, and then Jeff and Kate each had a message, too. Yes, somehow they both spoke at their own son's funeral. Kate's was from Job. Jeff talked about the love he felt for Colin and how God's love for Jesus was greater. Jeff would never have chosen to have his son die, but *God did*! He chose, out of His love for us, to have His Son face a heinous death. After they spoke, there was a photo history. Jeff's great-great-grandfather came to Kenya in 1910, and every generation since has had someone involved in missions. Colin had a place in that heritage too. Then they showed a video of Colin's birth and few days at home. There was great joy and great mourning throughout the service.

*february 20—in honor of colin

It was back in early December, and the three of us (Heather, Micah, and I) walked down the hill to the town cemetery. Heather's former co-worker at Santa Fe Christian in San Diego, who attended RVA back in the 70's and lost a brother while here, asked if we'd take a picture of the grave. We wandered among small stones, elaborate tombstones, and even some wooden markers until we found Paul's brother's. As my eyes ran over stone after stone and my mind tried to learn a bit about the people whose bodies lay below, I realized that nearly half of the deaths in this African cemetery were young children and infants.

God used this walk to teach me. You see, this journey happened concurrently with our nephew's battle for life at San Diego Children's Hospital. Our hearts were breaking as we wrestled with this dire situation. I felt God whispering on this day that it could be within His will to allow our nephew Christian to die. It had happened before to countless families, and this catastrophe would happen again. It could happen to our family. I didn't walk away with peace that day, but God awoke me from my denial of reality.

Christian recovered and is still recovering, and we're all full of praise to God, the merciful One who decided to save this boy, sparing his parents and everyone who loves the little man.

Colin Davis though was taken from his parents after just three days of life. He stopped breathing in his sleep, and two parents (and family scattered all throughout the world) lost their first born son. What should their reaction be? Can they praise the same merciful God, the One who decided to take Colin and not to spare his family and friends from this great sorrow?

Last week, I didn't know what to say to this. Praise God for this? How? What kind of lips could offer thanks for something so horrible? They waited for nine long months. They watched him take his first breath. They held his naked body against their skin. Then, they saw him lifeless. They held his unresponsive body in their arms. They put his small body in the earth. He was gone. What kind of God would do this?

This was my dilemma, and I think the dilemma of many touched by this tragedy. Amazingly, the ones who led us through this grieving process were the very ones who had the greatest reason to curse Him—Jeff and Kate. They quoted the key verse from Job repeatedly through the week, "The Lord gave and the Lord has taken away. Blessed be the name of the Lord." Their pain is great, but like Job, they will not curse God in this. They will only give Him praise as the One who knows, the One who ordains our days, the One who comforts and has eternal life in store. Jeff and Kate tearfully and forcefully commanded us, "Praise Him," and they had the authority to do so. If they were giving praise in this, they who lost their precious one, how could we not, too?

I wanted to rebel from their command, and I did most of last week. I love my friends, but surely they were wrong. Surely God does deserve some anger and blame in this. Surely I should stop loving Him so much and withhold some of my affections from Him. As last week went on, I sank lower and lower, felt my body withering away, lack of sleep, lack of joy, lack of hope. I avoided God, wouldn't talk to Him, wouldn't read my Bible, distracted myself from the situation. Until Friday night.

I sat down with my journal and had it out with God. And I found Him again. I found Him, even in this situation. I found Him the way that Jeff and Kate have found Him this week. He is sovereign, and He knows better. He doesn't waste any pain, and in fact, He's grieving over our pain, too. This tragedy has already brought glory to His name, has caused so many people to ask "Why?" of God and to seek His face more. But finding God and finding peace on Friday night does not end the grief. I cried and cried at his services on Saturday. I even cried while worshiping God this morning at church. We praise, and we grieve.

We worship the God who gives and takes away. Blessed be His name. Thank you Jeff and Kate for teaching me this brutally hard lesson. And Colin, I look forward to seeing you again one day in a body that will never die.

*february 23—ebenezer

My old roommate Joe introduced me to this word after our band played in a San Diego coffee shop one night. A recovering drug addict gave us a napkin drawing of ourselves with some words of thanks. Joe told me that I should keep it as a reminder (an Ebenezer) of how God used our music to reach the hurting. So what exactly is an Ebenezer? It's more than just an out-dated British first name to be brought out at Christmas time. It's actually a Hebrew word that means "stone of help," and you'll find its story in 1 Samuel 7:12-13.

The story is set before Israel had kings, and they were feeling like their lack of a visible ruler (God was supposed to be their king, but His invisibility made trust too hard for them) was hurting them as a nation. The Philistines (primarily) were constantly attacking them, and they begged their prophet (Samuel) to get them a king.

Before this happened though, God the King provided them with another commanding victory, sending thunder and lightning in the midst of battle to frighten and confuse their attackers. Samuel tried to remind them that God was the One who has helped them in the past, and so after this victory, he placed a large stone by a major ancient freeway to remind the people of their Heavenly Helper. He named the stone Ebenezer.

This was a visual reminder (a daily one for those who passed by this place with regularity) of a spiritual lesson learned. The stone wasn't holy in itself, and it had no earthly value, but what it represented in the relationship between God and His people was huge. If I weren't an English teacher, I'd call this here a good, old fashioned symbol.

Do you have Ebenezers in your life? Never really thought of it before? I'll share a few of mine.

If you read my story from early January about Ryan's pants, there's a prime example. Ebenezer 1. The hand-me-down pants of an old friend who died of a brain tumor serve as a daily reminder of the brevity of life and of the need to *carpe diem* for Jesus.

*ebenezer 2: praying hands

My grandpa was an inspirational man with God-given vocal abilities and kindness. His talents could have made him a rich man by worldly standards (he dreamed of studying voice for the opera), but instead he shared his gifts with thousands of people around the area of York County where he lived and worked. Ask anyone over 60 in our hometown, and they could tell you something good that Joe Workinger had done for them or for someone near to them. He was a difference maker in the places where God placed him. To mark our admiration, my generation of his family has middle-named many children after him, and I believe generations to come will as well. After he died, all I asked for from his possessions was a simple wooden carving of two praying hands. I doubt it's worth more than a few dollars to anyone in the world, but it's a priceless Ebenezer to me. To remember my heritage, I keep this plaque next to our dining room table, a stone of help.

*ebenezer 3: foreign Bibles

On our book shelf lays three Bibles which are of no use to us. You see, they're written in languages which we don't speak. But we keep them, not only to remember places where we visited and purchased them but to remember what they represent. Each Bible represents a missionary effort of time, money, and sacrifice to bring the Gospel of Jesus to people without it. One glance at that section of the book shelf, and I remember why. Why am I here in this strange land? Why do I wrestle with the challenges of another culture? Why have I left my family and friends? I teach so that others can reach the lost and offer them His invitation to true life. Foreign Bibles...Ebenezers on my book shelf.

*ebenezer 4: two e-mails

Our e-mail inbox. Yes, there are even cyberEbenezers. Last June, a deadline approached for us. We had about 85% of our monthly support raised for our move to Kenya, and we needed the final 15% in a few weeks or else we'd be delayed in leaving and RVA would have gaps in its faculty. We prayed, and others prayed for us, but we had no clue from where the money would come. Then, two out-of-the-blue e-mails shocked the socks off of us. Combined, the two made up precisely 15% of our support, and individually, each pledge was larger than any other individual's pledge up to that point. They remain in our inbox, the only old e-mails that remain with our current ones, as reminders that God takes care of us, sometimes in unpredictable and miraculous ways.

*ebenezer 5: photo of friends

The wedding photo on our wall isn't your usual wedding photo. Heather got the idea from one of her katrillion wedding magazines that she bought during our engagement. It's a "spontaneous" pic of our whole wedding party spread out in a line, from left to right, talking and laughing to ourselves, not looking at the camera. The photographer then used a fish eye lens so we (the bride and groom) are slightly larger in the middle and then the edges are curved. Besides being a very artistic shot, I love this photo because it represents quality relationships. Both of our siblings are in it, friends from our youth, friends from adulthood, kids that we were mentoring—all represent the richness of relationships which we were given and we worked at maintaining. Like the inscription on George Bailey's book at the end of *It's a Wonderful Life* ("No man is a failure who has friends"), seeing this hanging on our wall each day reminds me of the joy God has given me through my friends.

*ebenezer conclusion

I hope reading these short stories will help you identify symbolic reminders in your world which help you remember something about what's good in your life. You probably have had your own Ebenezers all along; you just forgot. It's the remembering part that's important. He was there yesterday for you, and He'll be there every moment today.

*march 1—where are the men?

We're a part of two congregations here—one is the local national church which was begun by missionaries nearly 100 years ago and the other is the RVA church which is primarily for the students and staff and is more Western in style. RVA church meets most Sundays while school is in session, but missionaries and students attend the local church during breaks and on the first Sunday of each month.

Today, while at the local church, something happened which reminded me of a tragic tendency in missions. On the wooden bench in front of me sat Matt and Kristy, a missionary couple, who were flanked by Andrea, Esther, Leslee, and Robin, four single missionaries at RVA. Matt in the middle with 5 ladies around him.

Now it's not tragic for women to be missionaries; no, it's quite the opposite—heroic, inspiring, righteous—especially when they go without a husband with whom to partner. The stories of single women fill the halls of missions history, and millions of believers give credit for their salvation because of those brave women who dared to risk it all. The first teacher in RVA history was Miss Josephine Hope, a single woman who responded to the need of AIM missionaries in 1907 to have education for their children while they worked with the unreached. Today, I doubt if half of the MK schools in the world could function without single ladies.

Where are the men though? This is where the tragedy lies, in my opinion. Why are single women a pillar of worldwide mission success while single men are barely an afterthought? At our home church in San Diego, there were a number of single women on the field and only one single man. When we arrived at our orientation in Africa, there were 8 singles in the group of 25 new missionaries, none of whom were men. Of the orientation's leaders and speakers, six were single women and only one was a single man. Finally, when we arrived at RVA, I was in for the biggest shock of all—12 unmarried women and 2 unmarried men as long-term missionaries.

In America, the Promise Keeper movement for men is still going strong, and the book *Wild at Heart*, detailing how Christian men could stop being nice and bored and start living passionately, has been at the top of the bestseller list for over 4 years. So where are these men? What is keeping them home that isn't keeping the ladies home? Do they enjoy the materialistic search for success more, the rat race? Are they seeking a wife more than they're seeking God's will? Are they cowards?

Woman after woman has told me that they realized going to the mission field would ruin any chance she ever had of getting married, or at the very least delay it. This painful decision was a lovely offering to our Lord, one of sacrifice and dedication. Rather than stick around and wait for Mr. Maybe and live a diminished life, they made a radical decision to go. And don't try to kid yourself that these are undesirable women, women who couldn't find a husband. These are beautiful, talented, and dynamic women who have chosen to listen to God rather than to seek out what "normal women" in their home countries do and what they have.

A new crop of single women are getting ready to leave for some mission field, even as we speak. They'll live lives of danger and sacrifice, joy and excitement (things that "real" men are supposedly drawn to), and they'll do it without spouses by their sides. I cheer them on and admire them greatly, but I must ask again, "Where are the men?"

*march 7—little language learner

Micah is learning Kikuyu along with us. Of course, his program is less academic than ours, but it is nevertheless effective. He hears Susan speak when she is watching him and hears us whenever we are practicing, so he hears a good bit of Kikuyu. As for speaking, we think he speaks mostly English. I say "think" because at this stage he's making noises and trying to communicate with us constantly. He's grasping new English words all the time, and we in turn reinforce his progress. But, if he's saying something in Kikuyu to us, we rarely can discern it. To us, he could be mangling an English word or he could be speaking perfect Kikuyu, unbeknownst to us. Here's a fun milestone in Micah's learning.

We noticed how Micah is categorizing the two languages the other day. He asked us for iria, the Kikuyu word for milk. Heather got him a cold cup full of milk, but rather than please him, this frustrated him. Near tears, he said over and over again, "Iria, iria!" Probing further, she asked him if he wanted it warm, and a smile washed over his angry, little red face. To us, iria and milk were synonyms; to Micah, they were two different drinks. Let me explain.

The Kikuyu people have historically not had access to refrigeration. Frozen foods and cold drinks… non-existent. Their favorite drink dates back to British colonial days—chai. (Chai to the Kenyan is simply any kind of tea, boiled milk, water, and sugar.) Chai, water, and an occasional soda are the extent of their beverage smorgasbord. If you don't have time to heat up your drink or if the sun hasn't done it for you, lukewarm is fine. Anything is better than cold to a Kikuyu. When Micah asks Susan for a drink, therefore, she gives it to him the way she'd prefer it—lukewarm or warm—even if it's juice!

Since Susan speaks Kikuyu mainly to Micah, she gives him iria heated up. Then, when we ask Micah if he wants milk, we give it to him ice cold out of the fridge. He's learned the difference. Iria is warm milk; milk is cold milk.

He's a missionary kid already, blending the cultures around him in his own unique way. Now if he could only teach his ignorant parents!

*march 20—a new start for joseph

You know how I got to Kijabe. Felt God's calling, begged for support, hopped on a plane, and here I am at Rift Valley Academy. Joseph's story is far more interesting, tragic, and hopefully, inspiring.

Joseph lived in a town northwest of Kijabe called Muru, a border town between his tribe, the Kikuyu, and the neighboring Kalejin tribe. He wasn't quite a teenager when one day he was out tending his family's goats. A truck full of Kalenjin men rode into his town shouting and waving swords and machetes. They began burning homes, killing men and boys, and hurting the women. When Joseph saw and heard what was happening in town, he ran into the "black forest" to hide and didn't emerge until the night covered him.

He cautiously returned to his home and found that his father had been murdered earlier that day. Everything in his home was stolen, but the home was not set on fire. He huddled on the floor that night with his mother, his sisters, his uncle, and another boy. They didn't sleep much, and in the middle night, the Kalenjin men returned. When they heard them coming, Joseph and his sister hid in the darkness of the adjoining room. The men came in, beat, and killed Joseph's uncle and the other boy. His mother was cut with their swords but was spared.

The next morning, they fled to a neighboring town where they were safe with other Kikuyu people. No one returned to Muru again. Without a husband, Joseph's mother Martha had to find a way to support her three children with no skills and no family wealth. Life is not kind to the widows and the fatherless here. Martha's story is tragic in its own right, but I'll save that one for another day.

Joseph was only able to go to Standard 8 in school since his mother had no money (students have to pay for Form 1-4 in Kenya, which is the equivalent of grades 9-12 in the United States). He's been mostly unemployed since then, working only a few odd jobs here and there to contribute to his family. He was able to go to mechanics school as a gift from a former missionary named Carrie who is now living in San Diego again, but there are still obstacles which keep making a career for himself difficult.

Joseph, now 20, stands at an important crossroads. We've given him a sizeable loan and gift that will pay for his driving school and the necessary mechanics tools, and yesterday he left Kijabe for the rest of his training in the city. Joseph's heavenly Father is watching out for him despite the loss of his earthly one. And we know that there'd be nothing greater than for him to one day be a responsible and mature father for his kids.

*march 26—rain and rest

We are t-i-r-e-d tired. Every term is tiring, but this term has been made even more so by the death of Colin right after midterm. The emotional toil that this took on the staff (not to mention the physical toil as people shuffled around to fill the holes left by his grieving parents) was huge. We have exactly three days until this term is over, and then four weeks of rest await us, so we're just trying to hold on.

The lack of a vehicle continues to frustrate. Our monthly trip to buy supplies was canceled because there weren't enough students interested to fill a bus. So, rather than a free trip to town as chaperones we'll have to pay $50 to rent a school car and drive to town ourselves. Luckily a rental was available on such short notice.

Micah's second birthday was last week. He had a *Madagascar* (the movie) themed birthday party thanks to his Nana Kuiper who sent all the party favors from California. There was pin-the-tail-on-the-lion game, King of the Lemur's dance competition, and animal-sounds Charades. It was wild, to say the least. He's growing up fast. He now knows how to count to ten in Kikuyu and how to spell his name and Africa; we're grateful for his life.

I was never a big fan of rain when I lived in Pennsylvania; we had plenty of it. I began to appreciate it more when I moved to San Diego in May of '96 and didn't see a drop fall from the sky for seven months. Rain was a nice change from those annoying sunny blue skies.

But this week, it's been a deep and profound joy to watch the rains fall. We've had a few days now of on and off downpours, and the dry and thirsty land is singing out "hallelujahs" along with the hurting people. This rain is long overdue. People have died, crops and livestock have died, and everyone has suffered in some way for lack of rain. Everyone is so happy now as rain is literally life for people.

SIX

thin air, thin pair

APRIL-MAY 2006

Another term of school has flown by. And because we're year-round, that means we have one more term to go. Graduation for our 70+ seniors is on July 14. March somehow completely disappeared. I graded 70 sophomore English research papers, Heather was named department chair for grades 7-12 Social Studies for next year, and Micah turned two years old. The day after grades were due, we began lesson planning for third term. The grind.

Our first visitors arrived on March 29th –Matt and Robyn from San Diego. It was a blast from the past to see faces from our "former life," and they have a busy month ahead of them sightseeing and ministering here in Kenya. It's been a blessing having friends here with us. Although transportation has been difficult (rental cars, trains, shuttle vans) and expensive, the first week has been safe and successful.

*april 5—the april fools

On April 1, Matt and I began a fool's journey—to climb the highest mountain in the country of Kenya. I was a fool because I'm not in top shape nor am I very interested in mountain climbing; Matt was a fool because he lives at sea level where the altitude is, well, zero. The trip was to take four days and all the mental and physical strength we had. Here's the story of our climb up Mt. Kenya.

*day 1—the line is drawn

We left at 8 a.m., 6 men and 10 backpacks of supplies, in a rusted out 1986 Pajero. The bumpy ride lasted 4 hours as we drove through one pothole-ridden village after another and past salivating thieves eager to get the backpacks off our roof. When we arrived at the Kenya Wildlife Service gate, the tops of the mountain were nowhere to be seen. Thick clouds enveloped Mt. Kenya's highest points, so we still didn't really know what we were in for.

Our porters arrived 45 minutes after our scheduled meeting time (which isn't bad for an African meeting), though just in time for the beginning rains. There was one porter for each of us (to carry food, cooking supplies, and clothing), one cook and a porter for him, and two guides. I thought that these helpers would be a luxury item; it turned out that we wouldn't have made it without them.

The first leg was 6 miles, all uphill, and on a rocky, muddy road. Early on, someone with a GPS reported that we were crossing the equator back down to the Southern Hemisphere; we drew a line in the dirt to make it seem more official and danced around it like freaks.

Our excitement fueled our pace; our guides and porters were shocked that they didn't beat us to Old Moses Lodge. Not even the downpour we hiked through could keep us down. We climbed 2,000 ft. in altitude that first day and slept in one of six rooms (8 bunks each) at the lodge. The night was cold yet bearable (45` F), but snoring men do not make good bedfellows. Of the four other groups, our start time would be last for the next morning—8:30 a.m. departure.

*day 2—our foe and our prize

After chai, eggs, and fruit, we began our second day—9 miles to the base of the summits. A clear, sunny morning revealed the peaks for the first time in the distance. The first portion of the day was a long, continuous uphill to the top of a ridge—about 4 miles total. With the sun still shining we descended into a small valley with a creek at its base to stop for some water. It was at that point that the weather changed dramatically—clouds poured into our small valley and covered everything from sky to ground.

Our porters got ahead of us this day and had lunch waiting for us by the river—cold-cut sandwiches and juice boxes. As soon as the last man finished eating (old 25-chews-per-swallow me), the rains began...heavy, heavy rains. With stomachs overstuffed, we made a brisk pace the final three miles, but it still took us two hours because of the muddy paths and bogs and the steady ascent.

Relief should have been what we felt when we arrived at Shipton's Camp; it wasn't. Not only was our current clothing soaked, but our bags had been soaked as well. Our dry clothes, which would have been great to warm us at a chilly 13,800 ft., were not dry. There was no fire in the lodge (just a cruelly empty fireplace), and the damp, cold air offered us little hope of anything drying by 3 a.m. the next morning. Yes, three in the morning was when our third day—the summit day—would begin. The rains passed by dinner time and with them the cloud cover; our foe and our prize was revealed from 3,000 feet above us. The distance, the terrain, and our individual, internal resources seemed like obstacles we might not be able to overcome.

We went to bed at 8 p.m., discouraged, cold, wet, and full of doubt over whether we could make it to the top.

*day 3—into thin and foul air

I wish I could say that waking up at 3 a.m. to summit was difficult. But, I can't, you see, because waking up assumes sleep. I didn't sleep at all the night before the climb to the summit. Call it anxiety or excitement or fear, but whatever it was, I couldn't unwind. I suppose it could have even been the altitude; I can't say I've ever slept at nearly 14,000 feet before.

Our trek to Pt. Lenana began at 3:30, and the clear, cool night that our guide predicted wasn't to be. Overcast, snowy skies greeted our damply layered bodies as we left the camp with water, cameras, and flashlights. With no idea of our course, we followed our guide's headlamp carefully up sharply angled paths. If I tried to look ahead of him at the ominous mountain, I became dizzy. If I tried to look down at the vanishing light of our camp below, I swayed and lost my balance. The only thing I could do for the 120 minutes of pitch black hiking was look at my guide. (I'm sure there are many great spiritual analogies here, but I'll save them for another day.)

I loved the pace set for us and really didn't struggle with breathing or with having the strength to climb. I mainly struggled to find clean air. I'm kind of a laid back guy, not the real aggressive type, so when we would fall into line during hikes, I usually let others go first, and I stayed to the back. On our assent, however, this personality trait proved to be a flaw. When hiking straight up a mountain, your head tends to be at eye level with the derriere of the fellow in front of you. No problem…unless the guy in front of you (or guys) can't stop releasing methane. With every step, it seemed like one person or another had the need to pass gas directly at me. I expected to be challenged on this summit, but not by the stench of my companions. So much for clean mountain air.

Snow covered paths became the norm beginning at 4:30, and the terrain turned to mostly scree (loose gravel and soil) by 5. Dawn began at a little before 6, and we turned off our flashlights with about 1000 more feet to climb. We missed our goal by fifteen minutes (to reach the peak by sunrise), but the spectacular sky kept prodding us on as we mounded over those final precarious boulders. Down one side rested a thinning glacier; down the other, the drop-off from where we just traveled.

As I said earlier, I'm not very interested in mountain climbing. I just agreed to do it because Matt wanted to, and well, what else am I going to do during school break? I wondered if the summit would be worth the money, the sweat, the frustrations, the fatigue. When I climbed over the last ledge and saw the 360 degree view of the whole of Kenya, I smiled. The first words out of my mouth: "This makes it all worth it."

I spent a joyous 30 minutes at the peak—taking pictures, drinking a cup of tea, eating the best Snickers bar ever, and calling my wife on my cell phone (somehow I got service there?). But on the way back down, altitude sickness started to hit most of us. Its symptoms—headache and nausea—hit Matt the hardest and for good reason. Everyone in our party lives at 7,000 feet at Rift Valley Academy; Matt goes surfing a few times a week at sea level in San Diego. He made it down the hill, but not without first throwing up and then dry heaving the rest of the way. By 8:45, we all descended and sat down for breakfast, a brief rest before embarking on the monotonous part of our day's itinerary.

The uphill journey that we did on day two had to be repeated. Although primarily downhill this time, it was long (9 miles and 5 hours), miserable (wet clothes, constant drizzle, and no sleep the night before), and tedious (the climax was over, and we'd already logged 19 arduous miles in less than 48 hours). There's not really much good to say about the rest of this day, except that maybe, since we all hiked alone and with more distance between us, the air smelled a little better on the way back to Old Moses Lodge.

*day 4—finishing well

Elias, our guide who had summited hundreds of times, set a late departure time for our last day—8 o'clock. We, however, were ready to go by 7. Getting a good night's sleep and a quick breakfast, we hit the trail for the final 6 miles back to the car. We clipped off a quick pace (15 minute miles) and reached the gate where we started by 10. Looking back up the mountain, the peaks once again veiled themselves in clouds, and we knew that the poor European chain smokers who had left Old Moses towards Shipton's Camp that morning were in for the same rough trek that we had.

The four hour car ride couldn't pass quickly enough as the diesel fumes and potholes of Kenyan roads battered our fragile bodies just a bit more. In my backpack, one dry pair of socks, my ankle brace, and a smashed Snickers bar were the only things that weren't dank, damp, and reeking. I was ready to be away from trails and lodges and vehicles and traveling buddies, too. I kept praying, "Finish well. You've run the race; now finish well."

I could set lofty goals, strive to reach them, persevere through difficulties, but if I fizzled out at the end, the whole achievement would lose its luster. My last challenge in the Mt. Kenya climb was to finish well—with love in my heart and patience in my exhausted body. I'd accomplished each goal on this journey, and now I just had to finish well.

*april 10—when God happens

Our sending church came through again for us. Clairemont Emmanuel Baptist in San Diego is where Heather grew up (and our friend Matt as well) and where I'd been attending since 1998. They have a crazy rich tradition of forming and sending missionaries, being only a church of a few hundred but having sent dozens of their own families to the field. They've been praying for us about the car situation and brainstorming ways to help us.

Their stop-gap solution was great. To cover the extra cost of rentals, they decided to give us an extra $100 each month. That took a lot of stress off us, knowing that we can freely rent the school's vehicle twice a month without making our monthly budget ache.

Long term, though, they found a way to donate $3,000. Sometimes when I'm dealing with such a large number, I lose perspective on how much money that is. That's three thousand dollars. 3,000. Dollars. Wow. Incredible.

Most things about this life of faith shock you when they actually happen. With human eyes, it's impossible to see a way. Obstacles, frustrations, and limitations tower over you.

And then God happens, and you wonder how you ever let yourself doubt.

*april 13—martha

    In chapter five, I shared the story of Joseph Githingi, the young man who lost his father and is training to be a mechanic; his mother Martha's story is equally compelling. This story is best told by a friend of ours who lives in San Diego now—Carrie.

    "Martha's husband was killed in the 90's in Rift Valley province in a tribal conflict, along with another child of hers. They lost everything...their home and farm. After that time, the family became refugees in different areas. They ended up in Mahi Mahiu where Martha tried to make ends meet, but it wasn't working and eventually she ended up in prostitution.

    "Well, Mahi Mahiu has a horrific HIV rate and that is where she contracted HIV. At this time, the girls and Joseph had moved up to where they live now, but Martha was gone all the time and the girls tried as best they could to take care of themselves.

    "A Kenyan evangelist came down to Mahi Mahiu and Martha knew he was talking to her and as she says, 'God put her on her feet and she went forward and said to the others, "From this day on, you'll not see me here again,"' and that was pretty much the case. She went back to her girls and Joseph and has been walking and growing from that day. I met her a bit before she moved back permanently (before she was a Christian) and have known her since.

    "However, from her various encounters, she had become pregnant and was fearful for the baby's health. I went down with her to get the HIV test and that was an extremely difficult day. Martha's HIV test was positive, but her baby (whom she later named Joy) is a miracle and does not have HIV. Martha is currently on antivirals provided at cost by the Kijabe Hospital through a program initiated by Dr. Fielder—a missionary doctor and friend of ours. Her girls and Joseph are all from her marriage to her husband and are all Christians. The eldest daughter's dream is to be a doctor in Kenya, and the middle daughter would like to be a nurse. Joseph has gone back to school for welding and auto mechanic training and has really matured. They are really trusting in God daily and are such genuine believers and friends."

Maybe you've never seen the relevance of the verse in James that says, "Religion that our Father accepts as pure and faultless is this: to look after orphans and widows in their distress," or of any of the other myriad of verses which address orphans and widows. In most of the world, those people are without a prayer. No legitimate source of income, no one to provide for them, and no hope. Prostitution and other illegal activities become their only options.

The church in Kenya attempts to turn the tide of culture, to have a heart like God towards their own that are poor and alone, but it has a long way to go. But it's not only in Kenya where the fatherless and the widows are pushed to the margins of society. We each have to find our way to be Christ's hands to these people wherever we find them, perhaps as close as our own neighborhood.

My friend Carrie has done exactly this, and it has made an eternal difference in more than a few lives. Martha may still be alive today because of Carrie's financial help and spiritual mentorship, and Martha's walk with God is definitely more alive than ever because of Carrie. That is pure. And that is faultless. And that is religion at its best.

*april 15—ruth, naomi, and a kin-redeemer

I was reading in the Old Testament a while back about the plight of two ladies 3,000 years ago—Ruth and Naomi. Ruth married Naomi's son, thus leaving her own family and cleaving to his. But he died at a young age, apparently a genetic weakness (or just bad luck) of that family because Naomi's husband and other sons died as well. Ruth and Naomi could've parted ways, striking out alone to find another husband or some other means of survival. For Ruth it would've been the wisest choice, as a younger and more attractive woman. But no. She decided to stick it out with her ex-mother-in-law. In the end, Ruth's feminine wiles persuaded a distant relative (who should've stepped up to help out earlier) to marry her, and both she and Naomi were literally saved by this kin-redeemer.

Their story was one I'd read before, but now that I've lived in this culture a while, I think I can understand it better. A woman in Kenya, without education or strength to labor, has little means to support herself. She needs a man to make ends meet…no, actually to survive.

Case in point—Martha's story. Without her husband, she had little option but to turn to prostitution. This sinful choice eventually broke her heart and brought her to the Lord. And God has provided for her through Carrie and Carrie's church. But without God, it's a tragedy, and millions of ladies in this country are living out tragic existences every day.

The story of Ruth is a miracle when you consider what could've happened. She could've traded her faith, abandoned Naomi, and destroyed herself through prostitution or illicit relationships. And in destroying herself, she would've lost the beautiful future God wanted for her. King David came from her branch of the tree, and the Savior of the world and the Jewish Messiah came from David's branch. God saw the abandoned woman, powerless and alone in a culture that forsook her, and came to her side. Lifted her up. Made her story great.

And God sees women like Martha today and does the same thing.

*april 19—the first born son

I just finished doing dishes in the kitchen, and I found myself crying. No, I'm not a big fan of doing dishes, but it wasn't that which broke me down. The song on the CD player while I washed was a first person telling of Abraham's story called "Holy is the Lord" by Andrew Peterson. The lyrics spoke of Abraham's painful obedience when God asked him to

sacrifice the very same child whom he had been promised and
for whom he had waited 90 years.

So take me to the mountain/I will follow where You lead
There I'll lay the body/of the boy You gave to me
And even though You take him/still I ever will obey
But Maker of this mountain, please/make another way

Holy is the Lord, holy is the Lord/and the Lord I will
obey
Lord, help me I don't know the way

Raw. That's how this song found me. Not only did our
close friends, the Davises, lose their little baby just two months
ago, but two more tragedies struck our community recently.

A ten year old boy, whose parents are missionaries in
Nairobi, ran into his bedroom on a Monday morning to practice
his saxophone. As he ran past the doorknob, his saxophone
strap caught on the door and dropped him to the floor,
temporarily unconscious. No one heard him fall though, and
the strap wrapped around his neck cut the oxygen off from his
body. When found shortly afterward, his parents could not
revive him. He died of asphyxiation.

I couldn't sleep the night I heard about the tragedy.
Visions of this brutal death kept going through my head, and
my heart empathized with the parents who lost their first born
son. Colin's death was as "natural" as death can be; his body
stopped breathing for no apparent reason. This death was as
horrific of an accidental death as I can imagine.

The powerlessness of the parents is so painfully evident,
both in a SIDS death and in a freak accident like this; neither
could be prevented in any way. The pain of loss was more than
I could fathom. I fought the whole night through, wrestling
with God over the same question of just two months ago: Is
God good?

A few days later, our nanny Susan came to work in
tears. While walking to work, she received news of a brutal

crime against her family. Her aunt and uncle were beaten and robbed the night before, but that wasn't the worst part. After the robbers left their house, they went next door to their son's place. He refused to let them in, so they beat down his door with an axe. Then, they continued using the axe on him and beat him until he was dead. The parents went to the hospital not knowing that their oldest son had even been harmed; later that morning they found out that he was dead.

You see, I have a two year old son, our first born, and I guess you could say that these recent passings have uncovered my deepest fear. If God took their sons, He could take mine. Micah is not "safe," I cannot protect him. His life is not in my hands; it's in the hands of the God who sometimes takes precious first born sons.

I talked a tough game on this issue. When people heard about us going to Africa, many said, "Aren't you afraid for Micah? Disease, violence, lions, and such?" I found myself parroting again and again, with much bravado: "His life is in God's hands. I'm not in control." I don't know if I fooled anyone else as much as I was fooling myself, but fears definitely lurked beneath my "faith talk." It's even in the chorus of the lullaby I wrote for Micah before he was born. The chorus goes, "My hopes for you are higher than the stars in the blue heaven/ But my hold on you is smaller than the breath that I've been given tonight/ So breathe tonight, breathe tonight." By singing that to him every night, I guess I'm trying to remind myself that he's not mine, that he's just been given to me for a while.

I don't think I'm really getting the message yet after singing it over 700 times because tonight I cried while doing the dishes. The conversation went like this.

"Do you love me more than your possessions?"
"Of course, Lord. They all belong to you."
"Than your life?"
"Take my life, Lord. It's yours."
"Do you love me more than you love your son?"

"Don't ask me that, Lord. Please, don't ask me that."

Yet he asked Abraham that, and Abraham honored him. He asked Jeff Davis that, and Jeff honored him. He asked the father in Nairobi that question, and he honored him through his ten year old's death. He asked Susan's uncle, and he too, believing that God is over all, honored the Lord. You could even say that God the Father asked it of Himself when He sent Jesus to be the sin offering for us. He listened from heaven to the screams and cries of His tortured Son on the cross, yet still He left him there to die alone because of His love for us. God the Father lost His first born Son, the only begotten Son.

What can I say to those examples? Who am I to debate the ways of God? What can I do but cry and weep and put my son on that same altar which Abraham did?

*april 25—are we there yet?

In chapter three, I wrote about the top 10 indicators that you are feeling at home at Rift Valley Academy. You probably had no clue what some of them meant, so as a means of explaining each one and updating you on how "at home" we feel, I'll elaborate on each one.

10. **Your white sneakers are the same color as everyone else's.** This place transformed from a bog to a dust bowl to a bog in the past nine months. The dry season brought dust blowing into every nook and cranny of life here. I had dust inside my wallet. Then, it began to rain in February, and now the bottom of everyone's pants are deep brown. Yes, my sneakers are dirty, but I was forewarned…don't bring white shoes. My grey sneakers and my brown dress shoes are holding up well.

9. **You know what all the keys on your key ring are for.** I got smart during last break. I separated my 21 old-fashioned skeleton keys onto two chains. One set for school and campus…the other for our house. Of course, while school's in session I must carry around all four pounds of keys, but at least I'll cut that load in half during our next school

break. I do know what they're all for, but it takes me at least fifteen seconds to locate the right one.

8. **You figure out how to flush your own toilet**. I got this one down pretty early on. You lift then hold down the handle for about four seconds, then release. If it doesn't catch the first time, you might need to try again. Four seconds usually lets the perfect amount of water into the bowl. Unfortunately though, going to other houses is made difficult because of this RVA quirk. Haven't we all born the embarrassment of a temperamental commode while visiting a neighbor? Yet, we still blush when it happens twice a week here.

7. **You are territorial about your seat during chai time**. Every day there is a fifteen minute chapel and a fifteen minute "chai" break for faculty and students. The faculty meets in the "chai room" and eats a snack, drinks chai or coffee, and shares prayer requests. Around the edges of the room are padded benches, and the middle of the room has padded chairs. Benches were our preference, and there seemed to be unclaimed spots on the left side. Hence, that has become our spot, and you better not sit there. You hear?

6. **You are able to finish your chai before 4th period**. I was a little uncertain of etiquette at first. Of our fifteen minutes for chai, at least five minutes are spent in prayer. Are you allowed to sip your chai and pray at the same time? What about nibbling on some bread? I followed my conscience and allowed myself little nibbles and sips during the prayers, as long as I'm still praying and my eyes are shut. (I've also done the little prayer peek—come on, I know you've peeked before, too—and seen others working on their snacks as well.) However, even with that extra five minutes of drinking and eating, I still sometimes fail to finish it by the bell.

5. **You learn to save your computer work every five minutes**. Electricity here *will* go out once a day, at the very least. We have generators on campus to back us up, but they take a few minutes to kick in. Hence, for sensitive machines

like computers and LCD projectors, we must have a UPS (uninterrupted power source). It's like a giant battery (as heavy as a car battery) that you plug in so it will stay charged. Then, when the power goes out, it kicks in for the minutes necessary until the generator starts up. However, even UPS's aren't faultless. Saving frequently will protect you from a quirky computer, a network crash, or a broken UPS.

    4. **You remember to take toilet paper with you every time you leave campus.** I guess this one applies to women more than men, but many times "visiting" Kenyan friends or churches is an all-day affair. A Kenyan toilet, or *choo* as they like to call it, is usually outdoors and is little more than a hole in the ground.

    3. **You can still breathe when you get to the top of the hill.** We live at the very bottom of the campus so this one especially relates to us. Campus is halfway up the hill, and most of the dorms are all the way up the hill. I'd say that overall we can breathe, but it takes some mild panting involved. When I was training to climb Mt. Kenya, there were a few weeks when I could glide up the stairs and inclines, talking all the while, without losing a breath. Those days didn't last long, and now that school's in session again, I'm as out of shape as those two old guys on the balcony from the Muppets.

    2. **You've learned how to grunt "hello" in three different languages.** "Hey" or "hi" is probably what you would grunt on your way to the water cooler in the morning. That's one that we share. Then there are two that you probably don't know. "Jambo" or "'mbo" is the Swahili greeting. "Ii" or "wi" (both rhyme with say) is the Kikuyu hello. That's three. Check this one off our "Is RVA your home?" list.

    1. **The whole campus knows whether you wear boxers or briefs.** Well, we've been here ten months now. We do laundry about once every ten days…so that's at least 30 times that our underwear have been hanging out on the line, drying in the African sun and in the Kijabe breeze, for the world to see. So if you live here at RVA, you can just walk past my

house on any Thursday to find the answer. *The answer, my friend, is blowin' the wind, the answer is blowin' in the wind.*

*may 2—bad hair year

Kijabe means "place of the wind, and in the tradition of places that are aptly named (like Atlantic City, NJ; Boulder, CO; Eureka, OR; and Intercourse, PA—you may have to look the last one up), there is a lot of wind here. In fact, the science geeks on campus put up some kind of gauge on a roof and found that winds had reached 60 miles per hour once.

It's pretty much a steady, year-round wind, too. It lets up a bit in the early morning hours, and depending on which part of campus you're walking, you might find a little shelter from the contours of the mountainside on which we live. But it's awfully constant.

Wind is a nice thing when it comes to climate. It stays cool here most of the year, and even on the hottest days, that warm, dusty breeze helps your sweat to evaporate quickly and feels pretty sweet.

The wind can wake you up at night…it gets that strong sometimes. If it's accompanied with driving rain, forget about sleep. The windows aren't the only things that rattle when the wind hits; it's the trees as well. There are a quite a few of those, and when their branches and leaves get rocking, it can be hard to sleep. It's quite a ruckus.

But the worst thing is what the wind does to your hair. Forget about having precision styling up on top; the wind is way too vicious for that. If you walk out with wet hair, the gusts will make you pay with poofy, disheveled, and disobedient frizz. Even trying gel can backfire. Certain stiff breezes can take the most gelled style and bend it to their malevolent will. Pony tails tend to fare well, and so do buzz cuts. That's about it though.

Another added dimension to the hair problem is "Where do you go for a haircut?" There isn't a campus barber. (Could you imagine trying to raise financial support as a barber for missionaries!) My wife has done a fine job learning how to hedge my hair and keep the edges from getting too prickly, but her on-the-job training can't equip her fast enough for the unorthodox jungle that is my hair. Needless to say, my hair has gotten longer and longer and longer as our year has progressed.

And so there is more material for the wind to torment as I go about my daily activities. Each morning wet on the way to school my wet hair is "blow-dried." Every afternoon while watching student activities I'm further tousled and raked. Then in the evening as I head to meetings, my daily "do" is totally undone. Longer tangles. Funkier styles. Uncivilized coifs. My bad hair year blows on...

*may 4—"he's a kikuyu"

The third term of the school year began last week, and I've been spending a lot of time in my home away from home (the copy room) and with my new family (the photocopier, paper cutter, and scissors).

The copy room in the morning is always a hectic place in the world of teachers. Gladys, a local lady who works in the office, handles the pressure of frantic teachers and temperamental copy machines with the grace of a bullfighter. Another teacher, while waiting for his copies, was teasing her about not being fast enough, using some of the Swahili words that he'd been learning. Since most Kenyans have limited fluency in English, Kikuyu, and Swahili, Gladys traded barbs with him and blamed him for getting her day off to a bad start. He pointed at me and said that I arrived first so I must be the one who ruined her morning. She quipped back, "He's a Kikuyu," as if to say, "One of my people could never make my upset." We joked some more about our languages and then went on with our days.

Even if it was in jest, her bold statement identifying me with the people I came to learn about and acculturate with was a real feather in my cap. I chose to identify with them, learn their language, and live with them, and no matter how white my skin or how bad my accent or how far away I was born, to them I'm a Kikuyu.

*may 9—a debt free way to be

How much do you owe? I mean, if you added up all of your debt—college, house, vehicles, credit cards—what is the total amount? Is it even possible to live in the States without debt these days? We couldn't. One of the first things I noticed about the rural Kenyan economy was that there is no debt, so I looked into how they do it.

Banks help individuals get into debt by offering loans, but it's hard to have banks without a stable government and economy—both institutions which Africa has historically struggled to establish. Banks exist in Kenya, but they are not a must-have service like in the States. It used to be only in the cities you'd find Kenyan banks, but they are progressively popping up in the towns and villages as well. So how does the economy work if loans and debt aren't a way of life?

As I wrote before, relationships are currency here. Your network of friends and family equals your ability to buy, borrow, and build. For example, after our nanny found employment with us, her husband and she were able to save some money towards buying the legal right to the land on which they'd been living. Since they couldn't raise it all, they asked family members, former missionaries, and current missionaries for help. Our gifts weren't mandatory, but we understood that this is part of our responsibility in relationships in Kenya. When all of their "relationships" chipped in, they bought the rights—debt free.

Not only are banks rare, but the concept and practice of saving is rare too. Most Americans have a multi-tiered savings system in case of emergency or special occasions—bank savings, investments, retirement funds, etc. Emergencies here fall on your relationship network. For special occasions though, Kenyans have some creative solutions.

One is a good old fashioned loan. When there are Westerners around who do have savings, that means that there is money available to borrow. Africans are generally good at repaying loans if they have jobs; when the month's paycheck comes in, they pay the amount agreed upon right off the top. What they don't have, they can't spend. The loan gets repaid, they'll have enough to live on for the month, and barring any emergencies, their personal budgets will balance. They'll pay it off month by month until it's erased.

The second though is much more creative. I'll use my Kenyan friend John Maina as an example. John has nine brothers and sisters, so what they do is they each put 1000 shillings (about 14 dollars) into a "pot" each month upon payday. Each month, a different one of them receives the pot and gets to use it for whatever project or need that s/he has. John put a new roof on his house this year and dug a well in his yard the year before. Both of these projects would be impossible since personal savings accounts don't exist and furthermore each project's cost was way beyond his monthly salary. John, like each of his siblings, plans for the next time he gets the pot because he knows it's coming.

To Westerners it's a weird way to live. We live (or strive to) so autonomously in America; only closest family members ever call on each other for funds and even then it's with some strain. Yet here, economic dependency on friends and family is a cornerstone of their relationships. You are expected to ask for help from those closest to you, and you expect them to do the same. It's how you say, "I love you," and "You are important." They share economic burdens rather than allow anyone to slip below the weight of debt.

*may 17—stages of culture shock

Deputation is an important phase of the missionary life. Before you can go to some distant culture for years at a time you need to have a team behind you. Some members of this team will be people who have known you for years and years, maybe since birth. Some will be people whom you've never even met face to face. But during deputation, all of these folks come together and unite behind one purpose. They want to see your mission succeed.

I put that in the least "religious" way possible because not everybody cares about God getting the glory for what we're doing. Some of them want to see Africans helped. Some simply love us and want to show us that they're behind us. Some probably just thought I was a fool who'd end up running my family into the gutter if they didn't help us out each month.

Like I said before, our deputation wasn't a magical mystery tour of churches. It mostly consisted of Bible studies and small groups of friends. We felt at home with the people we shared with. It was a very George Bailey, post-Christmas-Eve-suicide-attempt-party kind of time for us.

One of our favorite things to share with people actually didn't have to do with us. (Have I told you before that we're not very interesting? It's still true.) Our mission agency shared a video with us about culture shock, and we loved it so much that we thought it worth sharing.

The video came from a short-lived National Geographic series called *Worlds Apart*. The premise of the show was to take people from completely opposite cultures and immerse them in a foreign setting. Watch them struggle. Laugh at them. Learn about foreign cultures. It's not cruel; it's reality TV.

The episode we showed was about a spoiled, suburban poster-family from New Jersey who was sent to a remote, arid part of Northern Kenya called Marsabit. Their pampered children almost went off the deep end in this Nintendo-less and Domino's Pizza-devoid place, and only the "chief" of the family (known as Dad in America) seemed to enjoy the experience at all. By the end, they learned some lessons though and even found themselves crying on the plane ride home, wishing they didn't have to leave.

The amazing thing about their week in Kenya was that they went through the four textbook stages of culture shock—the honeymoon, withdrawal, anger, and acceptance.

Honeymoon—the huts and spears are cool.

Withdrawal—talking about ice cream and pizza all day long.

Anger—the daughter tearfully screaming about the bugs, dirt, and food.

Acceptance—the brattiest son going for contemplative walks with the tribe's elder.

I must have watched this video a dozen times while going through deputation, and certain parts of it made me laugh or cry each time. This short video encapsulated what some of our experiences would be like in moving to a new country. We thought it'd be a nice taste for our support team to have of cross-cultural missions.

Of course, these phases don't come perfectly one-after-another. There is overlap. No one moves into the acceptance phase and then lives happily ever after in the new culture. But generally, these are the stages.

Heather and I have found ourselves discussing our progression at various times this year, kind of checking to see if the "textbook" version of culture shock had any application for us. I don't know. Perhaps reading this you've seen the phases.

Visiting Kenyan friends in their homes was amazing the first few times. Seeing how they live and what they eat and how they relax—very eye opening. And worshiping in their churches, in a foreign language and with indigenous music, was a true slice of heaven. Going with another new family to a game park and seeing many of Africa's unique animals was another little awe-inspiring event. We still have occasional "honeymoon" moments, but most of them happened in our first five months.

There have also been many times where we've turned our ringer off this year. Now some of that deals with not wanting to deal with students (not true culture shock), but some of it was because Kenyan friends frequently are calling and needing something. We've also had our fair-share of nights where we don't grade papers, don't catch up on our emails back home, don't do any language study; we just set up our laptop and watch a movie or a reality TV show. I'd also chalk up our frequent conversations about American food to the "withdrawal" phase. These really began in October and are continuing as I write. (Is writing a form of avoidance?)

The Kenyan trait that most angers me deals with money. Everyone I talk to, even people I'd consider good friends, has something that they need, and since I'm white, they don't hesitate to ask me for it. This is such a frustration that some days it makes me not want to even talk to Kenyans. Literally every conversation has some hint of "need" in it, even if it's veiled as a prayer request or concern. And then there are lies. Lies like "I'll be there in 10 minutes" when the person knows that they will not be there for at least 2 hours. And lies like "Those bananas cost 20 shillings each" when everyone else who has bought bananas before knows that they cost 5 shillings each. Yes, I'm angry. Right now I'd say I'm in the heart of this one more than any other phase.

I've had tastes of the acceptance phase. Like accepting that the electricity goes off a few times a day, and I may lose some work on the computer. And accepting that it's hard for me to connect with God at a Kenyan church service. And accepting that my Kenyan friends have emergency financial needs every few months and that they are grateful for any little bit I can contribute.

But there's still a lot that angers me. And there's still a lot that I'm withdrawing from. And there are even things that amaze and exhilarate me about this culture from time to time as well.

I knew about all of these stages back during deputation, but you never know just how they'll affect you until you're here.

*may 26—food foibles

A student walked into my second period class at the beginning of the new school term, a new student presumably. I greeted him, and he acted like he knew me, smiling familiarly and seeming awfully at ease with all of the others. Intrigued, I examined his face a bit more closely. It was Josh! I did know this student. He was in my class first term, but what happened to him? Something was different.

Josh went on furlough (or home assignment) with his parents for four months, traveling to see churches and family in Switzerland, Canada, and California. Those places probably have many things in common, but for Josh, there was only one—good food. He ate burgers and donuts and pizza. And then he did it again. And again. He enjoyed his time away from Africa, and as a teenage boy, he didn't mind the hefty consequences.

Excessive wealth and food production are not calling cards of Kenya historically, and so the cuisine (by Western standards) is seriously lacking. Our first taste (excuse the pun) of this came at our Africa Based Orientation in July. We ate at a college cafeteria alongside the Kenyan students. Rice and beef stew. Then potatoes and beef stew. Then chapatis (like a tortilla) and beef stew. That was our lunch/dinner rotation. Did we have beef stew for breakfast too? No, silly, not for breakfast. We had bread and jam every day for breakfast. Yes, every day.

This went on for three weeks. Heather stopped attending the meals with me, and even our nutritionally-gifted son wouldn't eat at times. The lack of variety killed us. We were used to Chinese food for lunch, Mexican for dinner, Italian the next day, and American the day after that. Lots of fast food, lots of preservatives, and lots of flavor. Then suddenly our diet became lean, lean, lean and Kenyan, Kenyan, Kenyan. Every meal, every day. We didn't have access to a scale during that time, but I know our weight loss began then.

I never realized how important food is to your sense of security and well-being. Food is familiar, it makes your stomach feel nice, and it's an essential part of your morning, noon, and night. We were really thrown off kilter by the change in diet, and things didn't improve too much after we got to RVA.

*may 30—the biggest loser

The first foods we began to prepare and eat when we got to Rift Valley Academy were still different, even if we did incorporate some variety again. However, finding out what was available and what we could prepare here took time. We slowly began to find "normal" meals that would restore some sense of normalcy which had been lost the first few months. None of them, however, is as tasty as what we were used to in the States.

The meals we do eat now may not be very tasty, but they're not very fatty and include very few preservatives. It's also been a drastic health improvement wiping out fast food completely from our diet. Heather probably burns every calorie she eats during dinner simply by making every meal from scratch. And many nights making the meal turns out to be a two hour workout.

Calorie intake has plummeted while we've been here and overall activity has soared. Instead of walking 200 feet to my car, then driving for 15 minutes to get anywhere, and then walking another 200 feet from the parking lot, we now walk 5-10 minutes to get anywhere. When you add it up for an entire day, it's quite a bit of exercise.

Put exercise together with a healthy diet and what do you get? Weight loss. And this campus is full of losers. I've lost 10 pounds this year, and Heather's lost 20. One girl, who put on the infamous "Furlough 15" last fall in America, has already lost 10 pounds in the last 4 months. Our friend Heidi got so encouraged by the change in lifestyle here that she decided to be more deliberate about it. She went on an even more careful diet and added some jogging to lose over 30 pounds!

Don't get too jealous, though. What I gain in pants that are too loose (belts were always just an accessory before, never really a necessity) you gain in fabulous foods full of flavor. What I gain in healthy digestion you gain in faster food preparation. What I gain in lower cholesterol and lower risk for heart disease you gain in a McDonald's on every corner. Those may not seem like an advantage for you, but I'd trade you a glowing physical from the doctor for an extra large fry and a quarter pounder with cheese in a heartbeat.

My time will come. Home assignment will be here in just three short years. Then, like Josh, I too will be able to watch the fat come back on to my body like an extra large Pizza Hut pizza dripping its cheese greasily onto a paper plate. I will be a loser no more.

SEVEN

stranger year

As I walk across campus each day, I see hundreds of faces. After almost a year here, you'd expect most of those faces to begin looking familiar, wouldn't you? We're not in the middle of a bustling city. We live in a village of a few thousand people with thousands more in outlying rural areas. The campus and student body is fixed in number. But yet, every day, I see so many strangers. And I see so many eyes scan over my face and label me a stranger as well.

I thought by now I wouldn't be a stranger. Not after a year.

I always thought the theme song for *Cheers* would be a great song to sing at church. I know, I know. It's a TV show about slackers drinking beer and lusting after women. But that song...man, they nail it on the head. Community, belonging, fellowship. We need it so badly.

Sometimes you wanna go where everybody knows your name. And they're always glad you came. You wanna be where you can see your troubles are all the same. You wanna go where everybody knows your name.

Do you know what I mean?

To be known, not just by a person or two, not just by most of the people, but by everybody. I'm talking about not being a stranger anymore.

I'm talking about being home—where nothing is unfamiliar and nothing is unknown. It's a good feeling.

Kicking your shoes off. Not worrying about anything. Comfort. That's what I'm wanting.

Now before I go any further, I know that being a stranger is our reality here. The apostle Peter called us aliens and strangers in his first letter. Paul said we were far away from home in Galatians. Nowhere is home as long as we're on earth. Heaven is the home we're made for. Being a stranger is the essence of life in flesh.

I also know that no one ever will know me so well that every little piece of me will be familiar. There's always going to be a piece of me that's strange. Even to my best friend. Even to my wife. I will always be unknown to everyone but my Creator.

And I know that no place will ever feel so comfortable and so right. Sometimes I tell myself it's not so. It's called nostalgia, I guess. I get it for my hometown in Pennsylvania sometimes. I moved away when I was eighteen and almost immediately I began idealizing it. But then I go back for a visit. And there are things that are great and ideal (like the green, wooded hills and the small rustic towns), and then there are the things that are less than ideal, that don't feel right. The strange parts of my childhood home, like when sometimes people pretend not to know you and how few people seem genuinely content. Pennsylvania is not home, San Diego is not home, and Kijabe, even after twenty plus years of living here (which is our plan), won't be home.

Being weaned away from American life has been a tough process. The customs here are strange and so are the people. But because this is their "home" and their country, they aren't the strangers—I am. I'm a stranger, and everything is strange. It doesn't seem fair.

I guess I need to keep reminding myself. Home is an illusion. Everybody knowing your name is just nice lyrics. Being a stranger is our reality for this year and for all of our years to come on earth.

Until we go home. To our true home.

*june 4—a week in the life

These are just a few random happenings from our life this week:

- Heather gave a test on World War I on Friday. If you recall, this is the same history course which began with evolution and creation back in August. She's still moving through time....six weeks left to teach (yes, our school doesn't let out until July 14!) and only one hundred years of history left for her. This should be a breeze.

- I had a bad lunch on Thursday and was up until 5 a.m. Thursday night with...uhh...let's just say "stomach problems." I still taught on Friday (there aren't substitutes waiting for a call here) but am still feeling out of whack due to lack of sleep and lack of nutrients.

- The school had a 2½ hour talent show on Friday night. Music, dances, and I even dared to do a little comedy routine. I stole an idea from Conan O'Brien, making ridiculous predictions about the future of RVA. For example: "In the year 2007, RVA will electrify the fences surrounding campus. The cafeteria will then serve barbequed monkey for the next 6 weeks."

- Heather made yummy pizza for two students on Wednesday night, but our quirky oven burned one side to a crisp. The girls were so much fun though that no one seemed to care.

- I collected 75 compare/contrast essays dealing with apartheid in *Cry, the Beloved Country* and prejudice in *To Kill a Mockingbird*.

- Heather inadvertently found out that babysitting for others can be productive. Micah enjoys having a little girl named Moira over so much that he actually lets Mom do some of her school work while they ride tricycles up and down our dormitory hallway.

- Midterm grades are due Wednesday morning. "Midterm" consists of a responsibility-free weekend and then one day off for staff, as all students must leave campus for the three days.
- Two of our students, sisters Laura and Sarah, are on Cloud Nine right now. Their Mom is traveling back to Uganda from the US, but she flew through Nairobi so she could see her two oldest girls for the weekend.
- The varsity volleyball team is challenging the staff, and I've been enlisted. The game is Tuesday night, and I'm just hoping that my forehead doesn't read "Wilson" backwards on Wednesday morning.

*june 6—stupid calendar

It was spring of 2005, and we were wandering the aisles of Barnes and Noble, trying to burn a gift card before we left the country. Books? Magazines? Journals? Nah. Ahh, calendars! What a great idea! And better yet, there is one for 2006 with beautiful photos of our fine city, San Diego! Won't it be nice to remember all of our favorite places next year when we're in Africa?

Stupid, stupid, stupid idea.

There it is. San Diego's beautiful new downtown baseball stadium, glowing and full of life at sunset. We took Micah to his first baseball game there when the stadium opened in 2004 and sat nineteen rows back behind the Padres dugout, thanks to Bill, my mentor at Grossmont High.

Flip the page. Presidio Park, the gringo military establishment from the early mission years of San Diego. Our friends used to picnic at Presidio, and we have some memorable photos of our times there. It was also a favorite stop when we'd design car rallies around the city, like we did for our goddaughter Jessica's 17[h] birthday party.

The month of June has an aerial view of the harbor, featuring the cruise boats and the bayside resorts. One fall when my mom and step-dad visited, we went on a dinner cruise, and they invited some of my friends along, including this girl named Heather Kuiper. The first time they had met that kind girl with long brown hair and gorgeous eyes.

And the memories go on. All of the magical places where great friendships were made, where God rescued me from my self-despair, where I fell in love, where I was called into a life larger than myself.

What we thought was going to be a great idea, however, has turned out to be a thorn in the flesh. Every time we walk past those pictures hanging on the side of our fridge, the ache is there. Home. So far away. Physically. Emotionally. A year behind and years to go.

We should take it down. Or maybe not. Maybe we should experience the loss and let it be a part of our transition. I don't know.

Right now I just can't stand that stupid calendar.

*june 14—malaria

My wife interrupted my second period class on Friday. She had told me earlier in the morning that Micah was sick, and she was taking him to the doctor. Now, she was distraught and in tears.

"His lips are blue, and he's shaking. He won't stop vomiting. I need you to come now!"

I quickly arranged for coverage of my class, and although that person hadn't arrived yet, I told my students to finish their quizzes, and I ran out of the door.

As I was running (literally) off campus towards the hospital, a verse from John 11 popped into my head. "This sickness will not end in death." On the one hand, it was reassuring if it was a message from God about Micah's illness—"he's not going to die physically." But I immediately thought of the context. Jesus wasn't necessarily referring to physical sickness; he was referring to spiritual sickness and a lost soul. I thought back to the other recent losses, the firstborn sons around us who didn't live. Live or die, the message I took

143

away was "he will live eternally no matter what happens today." I took comfort in that hard fact.

I got to the hospital about 10 minutes after Heather and immediately knew why she was so upset. He lay there in the emergency room (remember, Kenyan's eerily use the name "casualty" for their ER) with blue lips, black eyes, and an empty stare aimed at the ceiling. His heart rate was high, but his body was freezing cold. He was a sick, sick little boy.

To fast forward a bit, he had the symptoms of malaria, although it was highly improbable given the altitude at which we live. The first precautionary test came back negative, probably because of the wild temperature swings characteristic of the disease. When nothing improved the next day and his fever went sky-high, another blood sample showed that he did indeed have malaria.

His fever subsided on Saturday, and we got the first dose of anti-malarial medicine in him. Zombie-like and unable to sit or stand, he slept most of the day Saturday. But the medicine was at work. Later in the day, the vomiting increased. He'd drink and then throw it up fifteen minutes later.

This continued for the next eighteen hours until Sunday morning, when his second dose of medication was due. Amazingly—I'd say miraculously—he stopped vomiting. If he had vomited up that medicine, we would have needed to admit him to the hospital for IVs.

He had signs of improvement Monday, but Tuesday was the big turn-around day. He ate more food, drank all day, and played sluggishly around the house. This morning (Wednesday) he woke up and jumped right on his tricycle. He's been smiling and laughing all day!

We're still not sure how he got it. If he got it two months ago when we were traveling at lower altitudes, it's extremely shocking and rare that it took this long to develop. If he got it here in Kijabe, then that's going to change the way a lot of people live here. As for today, I can't stop looking at his beaming face and thinking, "God is mercy."

*june 18—passing the test

We got another positive test today. No, it's not Micah this time. He's still doing fine.

This time it's Heather. And luckily, it's not a malaria test; it's a pregnancy test! We're expecting! What a great Father's Day gift for me. I'm a father of two!

She's starting to feel "different" in her belly already, and I've noticed she's much more tired. Luckily we only have two more weeks of school for this term, and then she can get some rest.

Alumni weekend (which includes hundreds of people traveling here from all over the world to celebrate our 100 years of ministry at RVA), finals, report cards, and graduation all happen in the next two weeks! It's pandemonium around here, but we're enjoying it.

I had my last guitar class of the year today. My two classes both came a long way, going from fresh beginners to playing in front of a crowd of people in less than a year. I taught them the power stance, the windmill strum, and the back crawl across stage. All of the things necessary to become a guitar god or goddess. What were once beginners are now virtual rock stars thanks to my tutelage. Wink, wink.

And speaking of rock stars, you'd think we were rock stars with our vehicle budget. With the help of a car agent, we've been aggressively looking for a vehicle around Nairobi in the $25,000-$30,000 range. He has a lot of good leads, and I've spent two full days in the city with him walking from seller to seller and test driving Toyotas mainly. It's sad how poor the quality is of some of the vehicles and how hard it is to find exactly what you're looking for. We're so grateful to be at the shopping stage and to have about half of our target amount for the vehicle raised. But we've been told to settle in for the long haul though, as many of our fellow missionaries at RVA have looked for months without success.

*june 25—good grief

Rift Valley Academy is lucky to have a great music department. We have a band teacher named Steve who leads an elementary, junior high, and high school band in addition to a wind ensemble, string ensemble, and jazz band. That's six groups! Then, we have a music teacher named Mark who leads all of the school's choirs. Mark also leads the school's Sunday morning worship music and preaches on occasion.

During yesterday's service, Mark stopped the music to explain why he chose the songs that he did. They were more traditional than we usually play, and he explained that he wanted to sing songs that captured the sorrows that we all experience. So many contemporary worship songs or "praise songs," as they are sometimes called, focus on good emotions. They sing about God's goodness and being happy and generally have little lyrical depth to them. For example, we might sing "You are good" twenty times in a certain song. Well, God is good, so there's nothing bad about that per se, but what about when we've been betrayed, when we've lost someone we love, when we're depressed? How do we worship God then?

The problem, Mark pointed out, isn't saying "God is good" when things are going bad. That's actually not a bad habit to be in. The problem is not being able to tell God that things are going bad, not being able to lift up our sorrow to Him as an expression of praise. When you read through the Psalms (the Hebrew word for "songs"), you hear David grieving and questioning God over and over again. Can you imagine us singing a worship song in today's churches that says, "My God, my God, why have you forsaken me?" Me neither. But David did.

And in fact, that's what ordinary people feel from time to time, but our vision of God is too small if we think He can only handle "You are so good" and He only likes our smiling faces that sing happy songs on Sunday mornings. Is God the God of good times…or the God of every time?

The last point Mark made was that every lament, every grief that is turned over to God results in praise. When we are courageous enough to give Him our hearts, in whatever state they are in, He will meet us there. Powerfully. Because He is God and He is good. And praise will result.

One of my favorite modern songs is "Blessed be your name" by Matt and Beth Redman, and I'll tell you why. The song is about praise, but the verses talk about praising God when life is unbearably bad and when life is overwhelmingly joyful. Then, the bridge section says "You give and take away" over and over again. Finally, someone is honest. God takes away. God chooses for us to suffer. God appoints seasons of grief in our lives. Instead of perpetuating this fantasy Christian land of "God is good all the time and I can't get this stupid grin off my face," we admit that life is full of trouble and smiling is not the answer to life's ills.

When I sing this song, I can't stop thinking about the hard things that God has brought into my life, the things I've suffered through, my losses—missing family, criticism of my teaching style, my nephew Christian's illness, Martha's battle with AIDS, the murder of Susan's cousin, Micah's malaria. I remember Jeff and Kate singing "Blessed be your name" at the funeral of their four day old son. The reason I make myself think on those things, however, is not because I want to wallow, but because I want my praise to be authentic. I want to praise God even though life isn't easy. Life is full of grief. God takes away things and people according to His purpose.

I want to practice praising God even for pain, and I think that's good worship in God's eyes. I think that's the kind of worship that will make Christians throughout the world prepared to minister to those around them. Not just the happy but the hurting. I think that's the kind of worship that Satan doesn't want to see happen. Like Job's wife, Satan wants us to "curse God and die" when grief comes.

One last anecdote: as a member of the worship team at RVA, one of our challenges is frequent power outages. It will only cut out for a few minutes before the generator kicks in, and it only happens every few months during actual church services, but still, it's annoying with mics and amps and PA systems and all. Some people don't believe in the devil; some people believe in mere coincidence and chance. But if you're one of us that does, you'll know that he likes to throw challenges and obstacles that thwart the work of God. The Bibles calls Satan the ruler of the air and the ruler of this present age, and so he has various ways to hamper the Spirit's moving. I find it peculiar that the one song which the power has cut out on numerous times over the past year is "Blessed be your name."

Sure, it could be chance. Or it could be that someone doesn't want us to praise God when the chips are down. Satan, though, is a defeated foe. What happens when the electricity goes off is even more powerful, more worshipful than when it is on.

We sing louder when there is no amplification. We can see most clearly when the lights are off. Our praise is most beautiful in the midst of our afflictions.

*june 30—how to make a thousand dollars

Late last night, I returned from my grueling journey, which spanned 32 hours, consisted of 600 miles of rough roads, and provided me zero hours sleep. That's the bad news. The good news? We have a vehicle! It didn't take us months and months like we expected, and considering the car market here, we actually got a pretty decent deal. The 1999 Toyota LandCruiser sitting in front of our apartment was imported from Japan last month and cost a shade over $30,000. The mechanics who inspected said it's in great shape, and it has just 35,000 miles right now.

When the deal was done, I wrote the largest check I've ever written by far. To my welcome surprise though, I made $1,000 just by signing my name on the bottom line . Got your attention? Want to know how to do it yourself? Follow along closely.

The first step is moving to a foreign country. I probably lost some of you already. I don't blame you. It's a whole lot easier to stay in the good old U.S. of A. Once you go foreign though, you learn a new currency. If you're a math whiz, you can figure it out in your head without too much pain. If you're not, you need a conversion chart or a numbers-loving spouse. However, this exchange rate does not stay stagnate. It fluctuates from time to time, and there are various factors involved. These fluctuations can be in your favor or not.

When the Kenyan economy is strong, then the dollar automatically is weaker. Therefore, we get "less" for our buck, regardless of how strong the U.S. economy is. When the U.S. economy is weak, then the dollar suffers and this causes us to use and need more money while we're here.

To rehash the past year, we got here and the dollar was weak and so was the shilling. The rate was about 76 shillings to the dollar. Then, the Kenyan economy skyrocketed while the U.S. economy slowly regained strength; this resulted in a 70-1 exchange rate for most of the past year. This is great for Kenya and its people, but not so great for us Americans. If a bunch of bananas costs 70 shillings, now we're paying exactly one dollar whereas earlier in the year it was closer to 90 cents.

Let me finally get to the point. Something has happened the past few weeks (U.S. stronger? Kenya weaker?) that has led to the exchange rate to climb higher. It's around 73-1 right now. This doesn't matter much if you're just talking about everyday, small purchases. But when you are exchanging a large sum of money at once, this difference is up in the hundred dollar range.

The second step in saving $1,000 is to buy when the rate is most in your favor. If we had bought our car last month, we would have paid a grand more simply because of the lower exchange rate. As it is, we saved this money by buying when we did. You can imagine our delight, especially in light of spending such an exorbitant amount on a car.

However, in this wild and wacky world of currency exchange, we could be kicking ourselves in another month if the rate goes another 3% higher. We might be lamenting how we lost a $1,000 by buying when we did. If that does happen though, I guess saving a dime on bananas might be some small consolation.

* july 1—the 1,001ˢᵗ friend

The first time I met our "car agent" he told me, "If I had 1,000 friends, now I have 1,001."

Before we could do any business together, it was important for him, as a Kenyan, to have a relationship with me. Never mind the fact that we knew each other for a whole 30 seconds. Business had to take place under the auspices of friendship. The old American adage, "Never mix business with pleasure," flies in the face of Kenyan convention.

Let me take a step back. First, a "car agent" was a new profession to me. Cars are so hard to find here and so hard to find for a good price that this service was created. Benson, my friend with a thousand before me, has been doing this for over ten years so apparently it's not a new thing. His basic duties are to call over town, using his network of used car lots, importers, and other agents representing sellers and find precisely the car his client is looking for. It's really no different than a real estate agent in the U.S.. Finding a house on your own, dealing with the legal issues and paperwork, and closing a deal is a lot of work. So it is with vehicles here.

My problems, if you want to call them that, with Benson began on day one, just a few minutes after it was established that we were now lifelong friends (tongue in cheek). The person who referred Benson to me said that Benson charged him nothing for his service. Coming from the States, this made perfect sense to me. When we bought our house in San Diego, we paid no commission to our agent. The seller paid for both their and our commission to respective agents. That's the way business works. As we talked however, I wanted to hear this for myself. I asked him how his commission worked, but instead of hearing what I expected, he said that he usually got 5%. I asked him how it had worked with my friend, the one who supposedly got the services for free, and he said that he only helped him as a favor to his friend who referred him.

Now, this is where a cultural conflict began. In the U.S., business follows a formula. Like I said, when you buy a house for the first time, your commission is paid by the seller. When you sell a house, you pay the commission for the buyer and seller's agents. The percentage of that commission is negotiable sometimes, but it will be discussed and included in the paperwork. In Kenya, there are no rules. Everything is negotiable. Nothing is fixed.

(To go off track for a second, negotiation has never been a strong point for me, so moving here has been a challenge. In a world where hardly any price is set, it's been a skill that I've had to develop. My first negotiation happened when I was 10 and visiting Mexico. I took a ten dollar bill from my parents and told them I saw a snazzy pair of sunglasses. They told me that I needed to negotiate the price, and I boldly said I would. I walked up to the counter waving my money, asked the man how much, was told ten dollars, and promptly placed the 10 spot in his hand. Quite a negotiator, wouldn't you say?)

From my cultural perspective, Benson was telling me the rules of business with him. He would not be my agent (and I did desperately need his services) if I would not pay the 5% commission. I agreed. But as the weeks wore on and I talked to other people who had done business with him, I began to press him. I wanted to know all of the facts. He disclosed little by little, and I came to understand that it's true: There ain't no such thing as a free lunch.

My friend who thought he got free services didn't. He was told he did, but I must consider this at best a "white lie." The price that my friend got for his car was a great price. Everyone says so. But what none of us knew was that the price would have been even better if Benson hadn't added his commission on to the negotiated price. Benson came to my friend and said, "The car costs 1.6 million shillings." My friend said, "That's great and I'll take it." In America, we'd think that the car costs 1.6, and then the seller is going to lose some of his selling price to pay the agent(s) involved. Nope. The "losses" are added into the price.

How much? I couldn't get that out of my "friend" because that's his business. I proposed a scenario to him: "So does that mean that the car could've cost 1.5 million and you added a 100 thousand shilling commission for yourself?" He said, "Yeah, something like that." Hardly a free service. Perhaps it was even more, and he was being careful not to tell me the real numbers.

Before the deal was closed I found out some more disheartening information. As my little network of contacts grew through this car search, I found out that 3% is the going rate for agents. When I pressed the issue with Benson, he denied it halfheartedly but kept emphasizing how great of a deal we got overall and how we couldn't have gotten it without him. He just couldn't understand the fact that a good deal doesn't substitute for getting a great deal and that getting a good deal with the wool pulled over your eyes isn't a substitute for clear and honest dealings. Another cultural difference.

I guess in the end, he was right. Everyone acknowledges that using Benson certainly saved me both money and months of searching blindly on my own. Two things though still irk me. One is that there are no rules here, and there is a lot of room for subtle dishonesty. The second is that all of this confusion and frustration came at the hands of someone who supposedly was putting friendship before business.

* july 2—dirty new kicks

Sometimes you do drastic things to get a good deal. To buy our Toyota LandCruiser, I had to do something drastic; I had to travel to Mombasa to pick it up. That meant boarding a bus at 10 o'clock at night and driving straight through until morning. Then, once signing the papers and dealing with the bank, we got right back on the road and drove back. Here's the painful part—Mombasa is a 7 hour drive away if you're not making any stops.

Seven hours on the road is a lot no matter where you are. Seven hours on Kenyan roads is a mugging. For some strange reason, the roads directly outside the big cities (Nairobi and Mombasa) are horrific. They used to be really bad and riddled with potholes back in the seventies. So you can imagine what they are like now—30 years later!—having had no improvements! You cannot go faster than 20 mph on any stretch of this road, which is not only frustrating because of the slow pace but physically painful because of the jostling. These terrible roads kept me from sleeping on the bus ride there and made me beyond irritable on the drive back.

The only saving grace of the trip (besides the fact that we brought back a vehicle to make our lives here easier) was the China Road. I suppose the Chinese government figures there is money to be made in Africa, and they need the trade route to be better. So, they're funding the repair of the road between Nairobi and Mombasa. The middle stretch is as good as any highway in the US. Smooth ride. 120 kph (70 mph) all the way.

But the rough stretches? Man. I haven't felt that bad since I was a kid with a new pair of shoes. You remember how it went. You were so excited to wear them everywhere; you may have even slept in them. Then, one day, it's rainy and muddy outside and without thinking, you've turned your bright white sneakers into stained and brown used shoes. That was the feeling. My new car…and I have to drive on these vicious roads? Painful.

* july 3—not-so-superhighway

One humorous note for the voyage—there was this amazingly long ditch along the China Road. I asked Benson what the ditch was. He said that they were going to put a cable with high speed Internet in it because Mombasa already had high speed (on the coast) and Nairobi wanted it (inland). Every few miles there'd be a small work team of about 8 Kenyans with shovels and one supervisor with a big jug of water.

The Stone Age meets Cyber Space. Eight men with shovels digging a 300 mile ditch so that people can Google for a recipe for barbecued Mongolian beef and for pictures of Tina Turner. Weird world.

*july 4—i tried

Back in January I confessed my inability to kick my addiction to American sports…specifically football. I felt really bad about it—the only guy sitting alone in the video room in the middle of the night watching an oblong brown ball get tossed and kicked over a 100-yard field. This past month, however, I had a chance to redeem myself. The sporting event followed worldwide made its four-year appearance in Germany—the FIFA World Cup of soccer.

A few weeks before the tournament started, my research began. I asked students questions about the national teams and bought a magazine to find out how the tournament worked. I tried to choose teams to follow and stars to focus on, you know, all of things I'd do for a sport I actually liked. I thought, maybe my feelings will follow if I just tell my mind that soccer is cool.

The games came on at normal times here (Germany is only a few hours behind us), so it wasn't hard to catch them on one of the school's televisions. It was a huge draw for the kids, especially since many of the teams playing are also "home countries" for students here.

So, you hear me pleading my case, right? I did a lot. I tried to get into this worldwide phenomenon that is soccer (football to them). Why am I not hooked? Why do I not even care about tonight's Cup championship game?

Okay, the first game I watched was good old U.S.A. against Africa's last remaining team—Ghana. Winner moves on, loser goes home. The game is tied at 1-1 when a referee calls a questionable foul on the U.S. player. It was inside the goal box so the Ghana guy got a penalty kick. No problem. Penalty kicks are basically free goals. Then, with the lead, Ghana spends the next 45 minutes playing all defense, making it impossible for the USA to score.

The next game I watched was 1-0. So boring. Then, I showed up 15 minutes late for the next game, and when I arrived it was 2-1. The next two hours featured absolutely *no goals!* Another snore-fest.

I resolved to myself—get there early. Don't miss a second. Was I rewarded with an exciting, goal-filled game? No. England nil-Portugal nil. Then, when it's tied after overtime, they have a shootout. Shootouts are fairly exciting, but to use them as a tie-breaker is like having a homerun hitting contest to settle a baseball game. It's such a diminished form of the real game. To make matters worse, England, my "favorite" team, lost 3-1 in the shootout.

I didn't watch the next round. Germany lost in another shootout. Lame game. Italy won in regulation by the whopping score of 1-0, but even that has to be marked with an asterisk. Why? Well, Italy has been having big-time problems with corruption among referees. Did Italy really win legitimately? The soccer-crazed public (myself *ex*cluded) will never know.

Quite frankly, I really don't care who wins tonight. I did my best to embrace this world passion but came up scratching my head. There's hardly any scoring, everybody fakes fouls, the overtimes are stupid, and the games are fixed. Sorry, about the negativity. It's a strange game, and it definitely makes me feel like a stranger while watching it, surrounded by the hype and excitement but feeling none of it. I'll keep trying, hoping for a change of heart, but right now all I can muster is a groan.

Long live soccer.

*july 13—milestone

We've finished our first year at Rift Valley Academy!
Grades are done, classes have wrapped up, and graduation is on
Saturday! Thank God!

*july 14—nosy right hand

I've been reading the chapter on hidden righteousness in
The Cost of Discipleship by Dietrich Bonhoeffer. He talked
about the verses where Jesus is talking about praying in your
closet and giving money in secret and not letting your right
hand know what the left is doing. Bonhoeffer puzzles over this
paradox. Be a city on a hill, be salt, but do it in secret? How
can this be?

This verse about your hands being ignorant of each
other's good deeds was always one I shrugged off as hyperbole
before. But Bonhoeffer is saying that our righteousness needs
to be hidden not to the world but to ourselves. If we want a
public audience, then that's our reward. If we want credit,
that's our only reward. The key is to walk so closely with God
that we don't even notice ourselves.

I feel heavily challenged by this. In our first year of
missionary work, it seems like part of our job is to "report" on
our work, to brag about how God is using us, and whatnot. I do
x, y, and z, and supporters pay for the work. Even here among
RVA staff, I feel obligated to do so much work in a week, and if
I do it, I'm done. I can rest and feel good about my work.

It's not that I never feel the Holy Spirit or that I'm
always operating out of selfishness. It has more to do with the
subtle meaning that Bonhoeffer is getting at. My right hand
always knows what my left hand is doing. Sometimes it not
only knows, but it compliments the left. Sometimes it holds my
left up for everyone to see, knowing full well that in the eyes of
the world, the left *will* be praised.

I'm busted. I'm convicted.

Since "letting the world see my good deeds and praise my Father in heaven" is part of my job description, I need a serious crash course on how to keep each hand's activity to itself. Otherwise, my selfishness is really going to screw up my soul in this missionary life.

*july 15—no attachments

A missionary friend in Lokichoggio told me recently about struggles she was having in her ministry. She is offering free nursing training, but the students lack commitment and motivation. She wants to provide them a way to provide for themselves for a lifetime, but they want to be given food, clothing, and shelter.

In her area, NGOs (non-government organizations) abound. Well-meaning people have seen the poverty and despair of the people in East Africa and have been moved to give. Their money supplies the Kenyans' basic needs and even some more advanced needs like medicine and computers. And on the surface this seems to be wonderful, philanthropic, and harmless.

But over time, these temporary solutions have become a detrimental crutch for Africans. The African worldview has traditionally been very short-sighted. Immediate needs take precedence. If wealthy and kind Westerners provide for today, they don't see a need to worry about tomorrow. So they don't train themselves, they don't work harder towards education, they don't build their economy and their infrastructure.

Without motivation to work, the country doesn't improve. Without improvement, new jobs aren't created. Without jobs, motivation remains low. What results is the clichéd "vicious cycle."

Our friend Joseph has attempted to escape this cycle of poverty, and we've been doing everything we can to help him do it. Carrie in San Diego paid for his mechanics school, and we paid for his driving school and mechanics tools. He's now a fully trained and qualified automobile mechanic. He's also still unemployed.

There are no jobs to be had for an inexperienced mechanic. He's traveled north to Meru and south to Narok; he's been to the capital of Nairobi and everywhere in between. One of the problems is automobiles are not a dime a dozen here, so there isn't a ton of work to be had. But the economy is good, the strongest it's ever been in Kenya, so more and more cars are going into circulation.

Another problem is the relational importance of African life. In America, we say, "It's all who you know," and the same is true here, but you could almost say, "It's all who you're related to" in Kenya. I told Joseph's story in chapter four, so you know that he doesn't have many family connections and doesn't really know anyone outside of this area. People will hire someone who is totally untrained and unqualified simply because they have a responsibility to their families. This leads to shoddy workmanship and service, and society suffers as a result.

Joseph has had two short stints of work ("attachments" are what they call them), but both were inherently flawed. The first employer agreed to allow him to apprentice at his shop for 50 shillings a day (less than a dollar). As if that salary weren't insulting enough, he put off paying Joseph week after week until Joseph finally quit. His second job was as a welder in a rural area five hours south from Kijabe. After only a few days at this job, the locals began to harass him because he wasn't of their tribe. Soon, violence broke out at the work site, and Joseph fled back to Kijabe.

I talked with him today, and he's very discouraged. He asked me to help him buy his own welding equipment so he can be self-employed, which is a very poorly thought out and expensive plan in itself. I don't want to perpetuate the "handout" mentality that is so problematic here, so I encouraged him to keep looking for work as a mechanic since that's where his training lies, to go back to the same garages and ask again if they need a worker. He said he wanted to go back to chopping grass with a ponga to make a few shillings a day. I told him to persevere with the skills he has. He wasn't sure what he was going to do.

He's trying, and he's motivated. He just needs a chance, and there are few of those going around.

*july 16—3 o'clock ghost town

When you do have a job, you can't wait until you don't. And for teachers and students at RVA, it's that time again—vacation time! The 400 students who live here nine months of the year have traveled home to various places in Africa, and the campus feels markedly empty. Sure, there are still about 200 people who live here year round (singles, couples, and children), but with no school in session, the heart of the campus looks like a ghost town. If you happen to see another missionary across the way, you throw up a distant wave and keep moving—kind of like a wary pioneer traversing through unfamiliar territory. What is this place which should be so familiar and why is it so quiet, so eerily quiet?

The national workers continue to work some days during vacation, so campus isn't totally lifeless during the daytime. You'll find them cleaning classrooms, trimming lawns, and running offices most of the time, but they have an interesting break time built into their schedules called "chai." This adopted British custom has fit in nicely with the highly social and laid back culture that is inherent in this African nation.

Workers begin at 8 and work until 10, at which point they all stop whatever it is they're doing and head to a common area to drink chai and eat a snack. At half past 10, they're back to work for ninety minutes until the noon hour when lunch begins. After an hour has passed, lunch is over, and workers clock in for 2 more hours. (Can you guess what's next?) The 3 o'clock chai break is also a half hour, and then the final hour and a half of the day wraps up the day, freeing them to walk, ride, or drive home at 5 pm.

It's inservice today, which means no students, a few faculty members holed up in some room or office somewhere, and national workers doing major cleaning around campus. As I walked across campus to use the choo (toilet), I noticed a classroom with all of the desks and chairs in the hall but no one currently moving a single piece of furniture. Then, a wheel barrow on the lawn sat peculiarly unmanned. In the staff copy room, there were cleaning supplies spread out everywhere but not a single cleaner. Outside the bathroom was a ladder and a work jacket, but its owner was nowhere to be found. Was it an alien abduction? Had the rapture come and I was left behind?

No. It was chai time.

I should have known. And I shouldn't have settled for a measly trip to the choo as a form of a break and then rushed back off to my lesson planning, not when a hot cup of sweet chai and a small pastry was in the offing. I really need to embrace these cultural differences, especially the ones that involve slacking off and eating food.

*july 19—the tenth life

The life and times of a cat in Kenya are hard. So hard it can kill you, and I regret to inform you that it did. K-K, the miracle cat, survived our son's body slams but could not survive the wilds of Africa.

Fighting with neighborhood cats was a common pastime for our little Siamese mutt, but we think she came across something a bit bigger than a cat.

We were sitting by the fire last Monday evening when we heard a terrifying cat shriek from outside and then heard something, presumably K-K, slam up against the closed window. I promptly opened the window, assuming she'd just finish up her fight and come in. Heather even left windows open all night so she could return.

That was the last we ever heard of K-K. No body, no sign of struggle, no collar. Nothing.

Heather asked around and was told by a missionary who had been here for most of his life that cats don't last long around here. He had 13 cats in about 20 years, all of them having met unknown or tragic fates.

The predator is still at large. It could have been a baboon. Or one of the campus security dogs. Or a Sykes monkey. It might have even been a bird of prey, as we've seen some gigantic birds perched on our dorm roof recently.

Micah's been asking about his cat less and less, and when he does, we're telling him that she's "missing" for the time being. That's what happens to all the toys he loses according to us, so that's a sufficient answer.

But our first African pet is a little more than missing. She's all out of miracles. She's on life # 10. She's a goner.

(As a sidenote: we saw our first rat in the house today. Perhaps our cat was busier than we thought when we weren't looking.)

*july 21—100% with an asterisk

I got a great e-mail from my friend Brian in San Diego on Tuesday. He got me caught up on his son's obsession with Chewbacca, the start of his wife's wedding coordinating business, and his hatred for paragraphs while e-mailing. He also hit me with a question. If I can paraphrase for him, it was something like, "Why don't you guys come home?" Good question.

You see there are different emotions that you communicate to different people. To supporters, you communicate your excitement for your work. To family, the ins and outs of daily living and family stuff. To people you live with here, your responses to different community events. And to best friends back home, you whine, complain, and mope. All of the emotions are true and real. I'm not lying to anyone. It's just that my voice changes depending on the audience. Each audience is equally necessary too, or else I might not be able to express all of the divergent feelings that gush out of my gooey heart each day.

So Brian gets the whine. Without Brian and a few other key friends, I would have to stew and simmer and percolate in my frustrations. It's not fair for me to dump on Heather or vice versa. Lord knows neither of us can handle any more discouragement or negativity on top of the other stressors. Our friends are a saving grace in that way. We need them, even if it is only in an e-mail every month or so.

But in only getting the whine, Brian doesn't see all of my heart. He gets purely the worst of my musings. And to him, it looks like my misery outshines the glare off of Donald Trump's head after a swim. So, he asks the question. *Why are you staying there?*

It was then I realized how lopsided of a picture I had painted for him. I quickly e-mailed back that despite the negative attitude at times and the hardships, we were 100% committed to our calling here. In our heart of hearts, we love what we're doing. Sure, the first year's been tough, but we are filled with hope for the future and are grateful to be able to serve here each moment. I felt good about allaying his fears.

Wait though. I said "we." That is my heart. I think it is my wife's heart, too. It's probably my wife's heart, too. *Is it my wife's heart, too?*

As I heated up some leftover rice and beef, I nonchalantly asked Heather where she stood with all of this. It's not the kind of thing you talk about every day—how do you feel about your life?—but she was ready to talk. And she made me glad I asked.

This year's been harder for her than she had expected. She didn't think "living" would be this hard. Cooking, cleaning, shopping, etc. Learning how to live is something you pick up through adolescence, but you have to relearn it if you break from your old world.

She didn't think she'd miss her friends, family and home so much. I knew this ache of hers already because she'd been looking for a way to take a trip home now for the past seven months. That and the fact that during every other meal here she'd mention some fast food joint with delectable barbeque sauce or perfectly salted tortilla chips.

She thought it'd be easier to make friends here. Although awfully independent and occasionally introverted back home, I think she always rested in the fact that her friends were there when she needed them. There's really no one like that—an emergency friend—at RVA yet.

She likes the school and the teaching aspect, but misses her first teaching job at Santa Fe Christian. She loves the kids, but finds it overwhelming living with them behind the same bars…I mean, fences of this campus. She's committed to our role in this whole mission enterprise, but finds the role very, very difficult.

I asked her if she'd agree to what I said about being 100% committed to our calling, and she said yes. With an asterisk. I love my wife's honesty.

The asterisk is she's depressed. She's been that way for the better part of the year, and I don't think the old pregnancy hormones are helping her out too much. The first year has taken a toll on her. And while she's 100% committed, if her heart doesn't change, if she can't find a pure passion for her work here, if the loneliness doesn't diminish at all, she's not sure how long she'll be able to last. Like I said, I'm glad I asked. 100% with an asterisk.

We talked for another half an hour about the future, and I tried to do more listening than fixing. I didn't want to play the spiritual Rambo and badger her into feeling the way she "should" feel. I respect her too much for that. She's a tough girl, and she didn't enter into this life lightly. The blues aren't going to bully her out of doing what she's made to do.

It was good that we communicated. We are one, but I can't assume that we're marching in step through this brutal parade. The same direction? Yes, and that direction is not home. We both know that.

Side by side? Absolutely. I could have no better partner in this missionary life. But at the same pace? No. As long as it's just the pace that's different, I think we can say we're okay.

*july 23—well, which is it?

Our life is hard to explain. Is it a difficult life full of sacrifice and struggle? Or is it a simple life, hardly differing from our former life? Do we describe ourselves as paupers scrambling to make a life or as normal Americans coasting through our enjoyable days of ease? Which is it?

Some days we feel like it's hard. The power goes out every few hours. We're on water rationing constantly. Groceries are an hour's car ride away one way. Even then, our meals are less enjoyable than what we're used to. An occasional, choppy, time-delayed, and expensive phone call is our only connection with family. A few written lines of e-mailed text are all we ever can experience with our friends. Our Internet is slow and spotty. We get stared at by all of the natives. We live in the worst apartment on campus. We have bars on our windows, gates on top of our doors, and barb-wire fences around our yard; there is constant danger outside, like theft, carjackings, and even armed robbery. Students walk into our house without knocking and expect entertainment, food, etc. Our schedule is so busy—with student ministry and relationships with nationals and communicating with supporters—that a genuine rest is hard to come by. Normal conveniences and freedoms, like a haircut or eating out, are gone. Bugs, pests, and lizards—need I say more? Sometimes I feel like we're suffering.

Other days I feel like a big stinking liar. How could I ever mislead anyone into thinking we have it rough? We drink water right from the tap. We have hot water. Our school has a generator so the power is rarely off for more than three minutes. We have easy access to phones and Internet, linking us to loved ones within minutes. We live within a gated community, and there are never less than four guards on duty. The air is clean, the temperature temperate, the weather agreeable. We've never missed a meal because of poverty. We have a nanny who helps us with our busy lives. We're surrounded by other Westerners, many of whom are Americans and near us in age. We don't have traffic, the 6 o'clock (bad) news, or telemarketers. I'd say we have it made.

It's a hard call. Compare us to the average American, we have it rough. Compare our life to many other missionaries, we're living it up. Compare our experiences with a missionary 100 years ago and you couldn't even associate the word "sacrifice" with what we do. This tension certainly wears on me when I talk with different people.

With our American folks, I struggle not to lean towards self-pity or not to take the martyr's pose. They tell me of trips to resorts which cost more than we make in two months or of delectable meals from trendy restaurants or of new luxury vehicles. I sometimes feel poor and wish for those same niceties. Or I can feel self-righteous and condemn those base and selfish desires for pleasure, which I've so heroically abandoned. The self-pitying missionary or the missionary as martyr—there is a struggle not to sin in either of those ways.

Then, on the flip side, when I'm hanging out with Kenyan friends, I can barely even talk about the lifestyle that I lead. I'm the one who is holding back the details of my luxurious living: our cell phones, our clean water, our refrigerator, and our laptop computer. I feel guilty for having so much and am embarrassed by all of my creature comforts.

How do I explain my life to you? It's not what you'd expect. It's not as stark and sacrificial as you'd think, but it quite possibly could be more spartan than you might like. There's always a tension in that dichotomy, and tension, it seems, is the name of the game when it comes to cross-cultural missions.

*july 29—you say goodbye, but I say hello

What was your life like a year ago today? What were your biggest joys, worries? Who has come into your life since then? Who has gone out? Where were you living?

It's been a while since we could say, "We were *here* a year ago today." But now we can. The first year at RVA is over—3 school terms, 12 months. We learned new curriculum. We began a tough language. We got sick a lot. We made Kenyan friends. Micah began making animal noises, then speaking in phrases, and now he's memorized half of the dialogue from *Finding Nemo*. We met new staff and then said goodbye to some.   Hello to seniors, goodbye to seniors. We struggled to get supplies until we got a car. We moved in, out, and back in. We'll be moving across campus again in December. A lot can happen in a year.

Micah and I just finished eating peanut butter and jelly on top of English muffins (homemade by Susan), a great way to start off these vacation days with my son. He eats almost as much as I do. I'd say he was going through a growth spurt, if it weren't for the fact that he's been eating like this for about 27 of the 28 months of his life. We're exploring a career in professional wrestling for him. We'll let him decide, but it's good for the boy to know his options.

Heather's still sleeping as I write, trying to make up for the night's insomnia and aches. She didn't feel this bad until the third trimester with Micah. But it's nice that she doesn't have to teach right now. This baby has four more weeks to shape up and then Mommy needs to have her body feeling back to normal again for school. I'm sure he/she understands that.

The rookies are here; the new staff for RVA '06-'07 arrived on Wednesday. We had a couple from Baton Rouge over last night for chicken, rice, and salad. He's going to be teaching in Heather's department, and she's an OB/GYN at the local hospital. It was nice to see that "Bambi in the high beams" look on someone else's face other than ours finally. Oddly though, it seemed like all the advice and suggestions that we made were empty. They're really going to have to learn it all on their own. No one can ease their first year transitions.

Tomorrow is my birthday, and I am going to be getting what probably will be the greatest birthday present ever. (Sorry, Dad, this even beats out the BMX bike when I was 9.) We have family arriving from the States! My mom and sister arrive at 8:50 p.m. on British Airways, and they'll be more welcome for my heart than the rain that's presently pelting my aluminum roof is for the banana tree in our yard.

Yes. We were *here* a year ago today. Heather, Micah, and I. Rift Valley Academy. Kenya. The missionary life.

It's been a strange year. We had various traumatic and exhilarating experiences beginning on the first day. During the layover of our flight to Kenya, we were within minutes of being in the middle of the London bombings. Then, we dove into learning a language which 99% of the world has never heard of. Our family grew to include Susan, our Kenyan nanny. We had our first commercial-free and family-less Christmas. We entered into the pain of Africa, living through a deadly eight month drought and befriending a woman with AIDS. I climbed Kenya's tallest mountain. My wife learned how to cook from scratch. Our son contracted malaria.

But no matter how exciting or challenging or mundane or depressing our life is here, our story is really unimportant.

God's story is what matters, and that's what missions work in Africa and missions work all over the world is about. When you become a part of God's story, it changes you. We're not the same after this year, but we're in the same place. And that's important for the work of evangelism here in Africa. We're part of a vast network of people supporting the work that the "front line" revolutionaries do. We teach the kids of missionaries, providing consistency and support for these talented kids, so their difference-making parents can be Jesus to the needy.

We'll gladly be strangers here for years and years to come, if that's what it takes to bring the Gospel to every nation, tribe, and tongue.

EIGHT

epilogue

**Very few people in our world are offering anything worth dying
for. Most of the messages we receive are about how to make
life easier. The call of Jesus goes the other direction:
It's about making our lives more difficult.**
Rob Bell

I had never heard of the word fellowship until I became
a Christian at 18. But as I heard more and more people use it
and got invited to more and more "fellowship" times, I soon
realized that I was a fellowship junkie. Always have been. As
a kid, I was the one organizing sleepovers, having little school
get-togethers, throwing pool parties, and starting basketball
tournaments. My addiction started early. Perhaps I was born
with it.

Even today I love a good party. I loved planning our
wedding together with my wife. It was like the ultimate party,
and we got to host it, write the program, pick the music. Even
our going-away parties were a blast when we left for Africa. It
was simultaneously sad and inspiring to see all of the friends
and family together one last time.

But now I'm thinking of another party. The party that
we'll have when we go on home assignment for the first time.
Two, maybe three years from now.

Everybody will be back together again. My dad will be
there cracking jokes off to the side of us. My mom will be
gushing to anyone who will listen. Heather's mom will be
following her around the room, soaking up every second she
can get. Micah will be five and sucking on the helium balloons

with his pockets filled with chocolate. Melting chocolate. Our other little one will be walking already, bumping into the legs of everyone in the crowded room and accidentally getting stepped on. But then Heather's dad will scoop the crying child up, and everything will be fine again

We'll have teriyaki chicken and burgers on the grill, but Heather and I will be so busy talking and reminiscing and listening that we won't eat a bite the entire night. There will be obnoxious music and some out-of-control games for the kids, many of whom were born or got really, really big while we were gone. It's going to be a mad house, a party like no other. Homecoming. Reunion. Fellowship.

Now imagine the party with only half the people. Now a third. Now a quarter. Imagine the party with only a handful of people there at all. Some homecoming. Some party. Who could be satisfied with such a party? Not me.

Now let me switch gears and talk about another party for a minute. It's already started, it's growing bigger, and it's going to be flipping wild by the end of the night. I want everybody to join the party. I want everybody to get cake crusted all over their mouths and dance to the music like their feet were on fire. I want the laughter to be so loud that you have to shout to have a conversation. I don't want anybody left out. I want everybody there.

Every tribe, every tongue, every nation. Joining together in a celebration thrown in honor of God. By God. Through God. You know I'm not talking about Ryan and Heather's party now, right?

God has a party planned for the end of time and there will be a representative there from every people group on Earth. How will that happen? Because you will listen and I will listen to what Jesus said and believe it. We'll let this good news transform us and we'll do whatever it takes to let the whole world know.

"Go and make disciples of all nations, baptizing in the name of the Father, the Son, and the Holy Spirit."

But the after-party isn't the only party going. The party starts from day one of a person's rebirth. It begins on the first day the first believer in the jungles of Papua New Guinea says, "I want Jesus." On the first day warring tribes in Ecuador share bread together because they accept that their enemies are actually their brothers in Christ. On the first day a prostitute on the streets of Calcutta says, "I was made for something better than this." On the first day someone dying of AIDS in Africa looks up into her doctor's eyes and says, "I want the peace I see in you."

The party is starting. We don't have to wait to join. I'm here in Kenya, doing my small part because I love a party. I wasn't always a part. I just got lucky. I got invited one day and came and now I want those who haven't come yet to come. This is where it's at.

*

Now, you've read this book. You've heard my frustrations, my pettiness, my weaknesses, and sometimes even my disdain for the missionary life. How do those parts of the book mesh with all of this "party" talk? What do pain and party have in common? Let me try to explain with one more story.

I was 22, single and about a year away from earning my teaching credential in California. I wasn't sure where I was going to teach yet, but I had heard about the need for teachers on the mission field. My church had quite a few missionaries who were working with unreached tribes, and I had gotten to know one of these couples, Bill and Donna, pretty well during one of their home assignments. So I asked them if they'd be willing to show me what their tribe was like and the MK school their daughters attended.

I didn't know what to expect when I got to the Philippines. I never grew up around missionaries. Most of what I'd heard about missionaries came through the jaded lenses of secular universities and Hollywood. But now that I was a Christian and studying Jesus, I went from vilifying these people as unbalanced, psychotic culture-destroyers to deifying them as the holiest of all Christians, the ones who sold it all like the rich young ruler and went wherever they were led like the disciples.

These were the monks of the Protestant world, in my mind. I pictured them with noses in Bibles and leading their children around like docile lambs and speaking in hushed whispers about the hundreds of conversions that they saw each week. If there wasn't a halo or aura hovering overhead, then it was only because I was too sinful to see it. I was ready to be in the presence of virtual angels here on Earth.

You can imagine my surprise when I heard one couple loudly bickering, when one of the missionary families watched 11 straight hours of movies one day, when I heard stories of MKs sneaking off at night to make out under the stars, when Bill played a Ray Stevens comedy CD for 2 hours straight and sang along to every ridiculous lyric.

Monks? Saints? Apostles? Try stooges, anger junkies, and hormonal youth.

These people weren't anything like I expected. In fact, they were no different than the Christians I hung out with in the U.S. or the kids I worked with at our church's youth group. Where were the all-night prayer meetings and the constant hymn whistling and the auras? These people lived just like me. They were average. Nothing out of the ordinary.

So if these people were no different, what would cause me to join their ranks? Why would I sell all I have, leave my friends and loved ones and the comfort of home to go live half way around the world with strange people and strange customs?

It's simple. The impact. They made an extraordinary impact.

Take Bill and Donna for instance. With their partners, they've almost finished translating the Bible into Palawano. For the last twenty years they've been teaching the people how to read, write, and interpret scripture for themselves. Big deal. You've heard of that before.

But did you know that twenty years ago, the witch doctors would tell the people to do things that would speed them and their children to their deaths? Did you know that they lived in constant fear of the forest spirits? Did you know that the girls were sold at a young age to anyone who wanted them for a bride? Did you know they felt bound to superstitions of farming and medicine that caused them to suffer for generations? Could you imagine the physical and spiritual pain they felt?

The good news of Jesus changed all of that. The party has started. They chose to believe, and they've had a thriving church—led by their own elders, not missionaries—for over a decade. They're going into surrounding areas, to other unreached tribes, and inviting them to the party. There's less fear among believers, there's wholeness in families, there's healthy lifestyles, there's joy amidst suffering, and the list goes on.

The impact of these normal people on the lives and the eternities of the lost blew my mind.

But Bill and Donna weren't the only missionaries I met. Going in and out of their tribe, I visited with pilots. And then I stayed at a guest house for a day and saw businessmen and women buying supplies for the missionaries. And then I went to the school where Bill and Donna's daughters went (a day's travel away) and mingled with the teachers, administrators, and dorm parents.

It took a team to make that impact. A team of ordinary people not much different than myself. They made themselves available to God, and He used them in such an amazing way that I couldn't help but give my life to that calling as well. An ordinary person (that was me) doing an extraordinary thing (that was what I wanted to do). I didn't know then where exactly God would call me to give, but I knew that one day, no matter what sacrifice it took, I'd give if God asked.

This is what I wanted, and this is what I want. I want to pour out my life so that some little tribe in Sudan can hear about the real Jesus (not the Muslim Jesus) for the first time. I want to experience pain and loss so that a Kenyan Bible student will be equipped to build new and healthy churches in regions no white man could go. I want to give whatever it takes so that a village in Tanzania will get safe, clean water and then hear about the way to never thirst again.

This is the small part I play in this team. Teaching the kids of parents who do various, extraordinary work to bring the party to Africa. They couldn't do what they're doing, the kingdom couldn't spread like it's spreading, without people like me.

Yes, even people like me. You know me, and you know how little I am. But please don't get lost in my failings. Embrace them. Know that this makes God even greater. That He can use someone like me to help the hurting and broken half a world away doesn't make me look good—I'm still the fragile, selfish, and confused young man you've been reading about. It makes Him look good because He's working out extraordinary and beautiful things in me and through me.

I hope my story has given you a glimpse—for better or worse—of what a real missionary looks like. I didn't try to put my best foot forward because that wasn't what inspired me in the year 2000. It's when we see an unimpressive and average vessel, cracked and worn on the outside, holding the most awe-inspiring contents on the inside that people take notice. When they see someone taking their lumps and forging ahead, then they know that the prize must be worth it.

Africa is worth it.

The good news party is worth it.

God is worth it.

ENDNOTES

Since I didn't really set out to write a book when
I started writing, this list of works cited is very
incomplete. Most of my learning here in Kenya has
either been experiential or via personal stories from
others. But if I had to list the sources which
provided me with the most insight, they'd be the
ones below.

o Andy and Deborah Kerr, *You Know You're an MK
  When...* (Watermelon World Publishing, 1997).

o Phil Dow, *School in the Clouds* (Pasadena: William
  Carey Library, 2003).

o David Maranz, *African Friends and Money Matters*
  (Dallas: SIL International, 2001).

o John Piper, *Don't Waste Your Life* (Wheaton: Crossway
  Books, 2003), 72.

o *Relevant* magazine

o Dietrich Bonhoeffer, *The Cost of Discipleship* (New
  York: Touchstone, 1995), 155-161.

- o Betty Barnett, *Friend Raising* (Seattle: YWAM Publishing, 2003).

- o Eds. Ralph Winter and Steven C. Hawthorne, *Perspectives on the World Christian Movement* (Pasadena: William Carey Library, 1999).

- o Rob Bell, *Velvet Elvis* (Grand Rapids: Zondervan, 2005), 169.

Lanny Arensen is the International Director of Africa Inland Mission, and I wanted to share what he had to say about Rift Valley Academy, the work of missionaries in Africa, and this book. His vision and leadership are a great blessing to the cause of Christ on this continent.

The Africa Inland Mission has been blessed in countless ways over the 110 years of its ministry in Africa. One of those blessings has been the Rift Valley Academy—a school for the children of missionaries. Charles Hurlburt, AIM's first general director, recognizing the necessity and value of providing education for missionary kids (MKs), founded RVA in 1906. The school started with one teacher, Josephine Hope and seven kids, in a small building with a dirt floor, no desks and no equipment. A building was completed in 1910 large enough to include dorms for boys and girls, dining hall and kitchen and classrooms. This building, named Kiambogo or "place of the buffalo" after the animals which roamed the area, still stands as the central structure of RVA.

Today the school has a student population of 500 coming from all over Africa and representing more than 25 missionary societies and many nationalities. The importance Mr. Hurlburt placed on family life and care for missionary children continues to be a core value of AIM. The number of second and third generation missionaries who have graduated from RVA and now serve with AIM, not to mention hundreds of others serving in other organizations all over the world, reflects the strategic importance of RVA. In recognition of that core value, AIM recognizes that a "calling" to MK education is as valid as any missionary call. God calls people to many different tasks—all of them important. If MKs are not cared for, the missionary endeavor cannot move forward. And in God's eyes each MK is precious and worthy of love and guidance. Therefore each teacher, each dorm parent, each administrator, each staff member comes to RVA only as they can testify to a strong sense of God's call or guidance in their lives.

This book is the fun and slightly mischievous story of a very "ordinary" young American couple who felt God call them to serve him by caring for MKs at RVA. Ryan and Heather Murphy are not that different from many Christian couples serving in schools across America. Except that they left their jobs in San Diego in obedience to God's leading and went to RVA to teach. This story recounts their transition from a paying job and a beautiful home in the United States to life as missionaries living at Kijabe, Kenya, and teaching at RVA.

Enjoy the journey with them and as you do pray for them and their colleagues and the MKs they serve. The story is not over and will not be complete until our Lord returns.